WITHDRAWN

Eyewitness Accounts of the American Revolution

Fragments of
Revolutionary History

Edited by Gillard Hunt

The New York Times & Arno Press

Reprint Edition 1971 by Arno Press Inc.

*

LC# 72-140869
ISBN 0-405-01197-0

*

Eyewitness Accounts of the American Revolution, Series III
ISBN for complete set: 0-405-01187-3

*

Manufactured in the United States of America

FRAGMENTS

OF

REVOLUTIONARY HISTORY.

Being hitherto unpublished writings of the men of the
American Revolution, collected and edited,
under authority of the District of Columbia
Society, Sons of the Revolution.

BY

GAILLARD HUNT,

Registrar and Historian.

———

BROOKLYN, N. Y.:
THE HISTORICAL PRINTING CLUB.
1892.

INTRODUCTORY NOTE.

A LARGE and important part of the manuscript sources of information upon the American Revolution are in the custody of private individuals. These scattered fragments are often the missing links in chains of important events, and until they are gathered together and printed they are to all intent and purpose unknown and valueless. It might be supposed that the people who would be most likely to have such papers in their possession would be the descendants of the men who wrote them, and it was a recognition of this probability that prompted the District of Columbia Society, Sons of the Revolution, to authorize the publication of such original Revolutionary writings as members of the Society might contribute. The request for contributions met with a prompt and satisfactory response. Some of the letters, it is true, have little worth from a purely historical point of view, but are nevertheless useful, serving to place vividly before us, as living and breathing human beings, characters that lived a century ago. On the other hand, others of the MSS. have a decided historical interest.

The most valuable private collection which has

been placed at the editor's disposal, is that of the late Colonel Theodorus Bailey Myers, of New York, now in the possession of his son, Theodorus Bailey Myers Mason, Lieutenant U. S. N., the founder of the Washington branch of the Sons of the Revolution. Among the letters which it has contributed to this volume are those of General Daniel Morgan, which fell into Col. Myer's hands when they were sold in New Orleans in 1879. "Some part, at least," says Mr. Winsor in his *Narrative and Critical History of America*, "of the correspondence of General Morgan is in the collection of Theodorus Bailey Myers." The whole of it, so far as it was ever collected, is there. It was used by James Graham in his Life of Morgan, and later by Colonel Myers himself in his account of the battle of the Cowpens, which appeared in the Charleston *News and Courier* in 1881. Taken in connection with previous publications what will be found here makes a tolerably complete history of the latter past of Morgan's military career.

Another contribution which must be said to have a decided historical value, is the narrative of Colonel John Francis Mercer. He tells how he impeded the progress of the British Army with a band of less than fifty horsemen at Green Spring, and again he engaged Tarleton's Army with great gallantry in the Gloucester skirmish. For the first affair he was thanked by Lafayette, and for the

second by the Commander-in-Chief. His narrative
of the Gloucester skirmish throws new light upon
it without disturbing existing accounts, but his
version of the Green Spring action varies materially
from those which are usually considered authentic.
It was, according to Mercer, silly and ill-devised,
and had the enemy followed up the advantages he
gained, Cornwallis would never have been obliged
to surrender at Yorktown. It is only fair in es-
timating Mercer's opinion of Lafayette's conduct
to remember that Mercer had been Aide-de-Camp
to General Charles Lee at the battle of Monmouth,
and that he had been the first witness called to
testify in Lee's behalf when the latter was court-
martialled. He left the army at the same time
with Lee, and did not serve again until the Yorktown campaign. As he sympathized strongly with
Lee, it is not improbable that he shared some of
Lee's prejudices, prominent among which was a
dislike of our French allies.

In the group of fifteen letters of the Lafayette
correspondence, it will be observed that several
sources have been drawn upon. Rear Admiral F.
A. Roe, U. S. N., has, through the kindness of
Mrs. S. H. Gouverneur, of Washington, contributed
several important Lafayette-Monroe letters, and a
few others have been taken from the State Department collection of Monroe papers purchased in
1849. Another letter from the private Gouverneur

collection is the characteristic one of General Charles Lee to James Monroe.

Outside of the contributions from members of the Society, the editor has in another instance had recourse to the Manuscript Archives of the government—this time to the privateer records in the United States Supreme Court. This was with a view to completing in some degree the story of the Scudder depredations. The incident is not one of great importance, but it shows how rigorously the orders against such depredations were enforced.

The groups of letters will, it is believed, be found sufficiently clear without further comment. Except those that have been described above, all came from the members of the Society of the Sons of the Revolution. GAILLARD HUNT.

Washington, January, 1892.

CONTENTS AND BY WHOM CONTRIBUTED.

---

* Through the courtesy of Mrs. S. H. Gouverneur.

* Through the courtesy of Mrs. S. H. Gouverneur.

GENERAL DANIEL MORGAN.

LIEUT. COL. BENJAMIN FORD* TO MORGAN.

WILMINGTON, 25 May, 1778.†

Sir:

I have received certain information that Mrs. Saunderson, a Lady from Maryland (who obtained permission from Genl. Smallwood to go to Philadelphia return), is to leave the city to-morrow will be escorted by several officers from Maryland belonging to the New Levies in the British Service.

I doubt not but you will endeavor to secure those Gentry who have given such striking proofs of their desire to enslave their country. It is more than probable they may appear in the Garb of

---

*Benj. Ford was commissioned Lieut. Col. 6th Maryland Regt. Apl. 17, 1777, and is presumably the same Lieut. Col. Ford, who, together with Colonels Williams and Gunby and Lieut. Col. Howard, had charge of the Maryland Brigade at the battle of Eutaw Springs, Sept. 8, 1781. Col. Ford was so badly wounded in this engagement that he died a few days afterwards. —Lee's *Memoirs*, Vol 2, p. 59 *et seq.*

†At this time Morgan was at Radnor, Pa., patrolling the country between the Schuylkill and Darby Creek.—Graham, *Life of Morgan*, p. 198.

Quakers or peasants and may be expected at Darby between the hours of 12 & 4 o'clock.

I am Sir Yr. most obt.

And very Hble. St.

BENJAMIN FORD

Lt Colo. 6th M. Regt.

Colo. Morgan.

D. GOULD TO MORGAN.

AUG^{T} 4th 1779 4 o'clock a. m.

Sir:

The treatment you this day very undeservedly gave me is such as no man ever has, or ever shall, offer with impunity. There are few men in America whose Publick Character I entertain a higher respect for than Col? Morgan's—and am therefore Solicitous to obtain his good opinion, nor can I possibly be satisfied he should think me so contemptible a *rascal*, as to put up tamely with his abuse—when Col? Morgan decended so much beneath the Gentleman in his unmanly and illiberal treatment he will please to recollect he was in possession of my Bill for 1000 Dollars. This circumstance (which laid me under some restraint) is now removed, and I can no longer avoid informing you that I feel the sentiment of a noble soul, basely injured, and have a right to expect, (if you are actuated by that delicate sensibility which ought to in-

fluence every man of true honor) you will not hesitate a moment to give such intimation to the company then present, as your good sense will natur-
ally dictate; but if this mode of proceeding is
incompatible with your [sic] I beg you will inform
me, how, when, & where, (within 20 hours) you
will meet as a Gentleman your most obt.

hble servt
D. GOULD.

Please consider sir that this paper was intended
to be delivered you in town, but when I had wrote
it, on enquiry found you had left Winchester, however shall stay at my lodgings till to-morrow morning 10 o'clock for your response. *

GENL. MUHLENBERG TO MORGAN.
FREDERICKSBURG, August 10th, 1780.

Dear Col? :

Enclosed I have the Honor to transmit you the
Arrangement of the Virginia line† as formed by

---

*After the campaign of 1778 Morgan, sharing in the dissatis-
faction with Congress which was prevalent in the Army at that
time, and suffering from ill-health beside, resigned his command and returned to Frederick county early in the summer
of 1779. He remained there until after the battle of Camden,
and in September, 1780, he again appeared in the field. The
challenge given above was received when he was at home.
Unfortunately there is no record of its sequel.

†August 1st the Virginia legislature passed a bill authorizing
the raising of 3000 levies. The duty devolved upon Muhlen-

His Excellency the Commander-in-Chief—and likewise a Letter from His Excellency the Governor.

I set out this morning for Chesterfield Court House to send in those men who are at present assembled at that place.

As soon as I get to Richmond, I shall send you orders for the officers in the countie which I request you to communicate—there is no news from the Southward and but little from the Northward.

I am Dear Col?.

Your most obd^t hbl. servt.

P. MUHLENBERG.

MORGAN TO GATES.

SALSBURY, 20th Oct.* 1780.

Dear Sir:

I am just setting out for Tephers, where my detachment arrived last evening. Genl. Smalwood de-

---

berg, Febiger, Greene of the 6th Reg't., Morgan, Wood, Gist, Daviess, and Bufords were the Colonels who had thus far escaped capture. The old soldiers had collected at Chesterfield, and Muhlenberg undertook to complete the regiments—a task which he had partially accomplished by September 1st.—Muhlenberg's *Life of Genl. Muhlenberg.* p. 197, *et. seq.*

* Morgan had been appointed a Brigadier General on the 18th, but had not yet been apprised of his promotion. (Graham's *Morgan.*)

tain'd me to go on with the cavalry—no certain intelligence from the enemy since the 18ᵗʰ They
were on Monday last nine miles beyond Charlott*
on the Road Leading to the old nation ford and at
or near steel creek road that leads to camdon—I
can't account for their nanuvers, as it seems thay
are short of provision & Forage and still continue
at or near that place—but must think thay are going to Camdon.

I am inform'd you are coming on with the main
body which I think very advisable—Salsbury will
be a very safe & comodeous encampment provided
a sufficient number of boats are procured at the
Yadkin well supplied with good ferry men and a
sufficient command of men left to guard the place.
I think if you can march a thousand men we can
act with safety, and cover the country—I have been
very sick since I left Hilsborough, but have got
well except a very sore mouth.

Being separated from Genˡ. Smallwood have had
little to eat or drink except meat & bread, no
stores were allowed me when I came away. Genˡ.
Smallwood & Mr. Pen told me you would see me
provided for. I spoke to you but through a plenty
of business I emagine you forgot me—I assure you

---

* "The King's troops left Charlotte town on the evening of the
14th to march to Catawba ford." (Tarleton's Campaigns.) The
defeat of Col. Ferguson at Kings Mountain had occurred on the
7th.

an officer looks very blank when he hant it in his power to ask his officers to eat with him at times— I understand some linnen is coming on for the officers, if so, would be glad to get some. I come off from home bare of them thinking to be supplied at richmond but could not get a yard, if I can get any my old friend Col⁰. Rosekranz * will be kind enough to take charge of it for me and have it brought on his baggage.

I have the Honor to be

With High esteem

Your obed.ᵗ servt.

DAN MORGAN.

GENERAL W. SMALLWOOD † TO MORGAN.

CAMP NEW PROVIDENCE, 3ᵈ November, 1780.

Dear Sir:

Having understood that the disaffected Inhabitants in the settlements of Lynch Creek, and Waxhaw, since the retreat of the British from Charlotte, have meditated the removal of their property to Camden, I was induced to order Colo. Davie with a detachment down into that quarter, to intercept all such property, which he might apprehend was

---

* Probably Captain Jacobus Rosekrans of the 5ᵗʰ N. Y. Regt.

† Smallwood had come to the Southern Department with Gates, and about a month after the battle of Camden was promoted to Major General.

about to be removed, and to draw what supplies of forage, and Provisions, could otherwise be procured, exclusive of the stock necessary for consumption of the remaining Inhabitants.

I have this day received intelligence that a party of four hundred British & Tories,* have advanced up to the Hanging Rock, to cover the disaffected who are actually removing not only their own effects, but the property of such Whigs as they fall in with, and apprehending the detachment under Col? Davie will be annoyed in the Execution of their Duty,—You will therefore proceed down with the Cavalry, Light Infantry, and Rifle men below the Range of his duty, to cover them in the discharge thereof.—March with all imaginable secrecy and dispatch, and if possible give the enemy a stroke at the Hanging Rock, should they still be there, and no powerful reasons against it.

---

* On receiving intelligence that Lord Cornwallis had occupied Charlotte, Gates detached Smallwood to the Yadkin, with directions to post himself at the ford of the river, and to take command of all the troops in that quarter of the country. The more effectually to harass the enemy, a light corps was selected from the army and placed under the command of Morgan, now a Brigadier General.

"Smallwood having received information that a body of royal militia had entered the country in which he foraged, for the purpose of intercepting his wagons, detached Morgan and Washington against them. Intelligence of Morgan's approach being received, the party retreated." Marshall's *Washington*, Vol. I, p. 398 *et seq* (2d Edition).

In accomplishing your views should it be necessary you will call to your aid any part of Davie's detachment, but otherwise, I would not wish their duty to be obstructed—

It will be unnecessary to caution you to guard against a surprise, and to restrain the soldiery from distressing such of the Inhabitants as may merit your attention. Your own Judgment and vigilance in the first instance, and your Humanity and discretion in the latter, will govern—

It is not improbable but you may fall in with part of our Tents, Waggons, and Baggage plundered by the Tories after General Gates's defeat. Whatever you fall in with under that description secure and forward to camp—

You will give me the earliest, and frequent Intelligence of your transactions, and as speedy as possible, accomplishing the views comprized in your Instructions, return to camp—distribute the orders prohibiting plundering, copies of which are Enclosed and it may not be amiss to give assurances of Lenity to such Tories, who may return and submit to the mercy of their country, intimating that proclamations to that purpose will be issued.—Wishing you success and a pleasant tour, I am, with sincere —

Your obdt. Humble servt.
W. SMALLWOOD.

B. BRUIN TO MORGAN.

GUILFORD COURT HOUSE, Nov. 1780.

Dear General:

I write to you, but with pain having no information but what must displease you. The Bearer of your Letters was severely beaten, and your letters examined at Taylors Tavern, within twelve miles of Salisbury by one Penny an impertinent Fellow in that neighborhood—I did not learn this, before I reached Salisbury or I should have attempted to secure him—A Gentleman immediately from Philadelphia assures me, that General Lincoln is exchanged for Phillips * and will shortly resume his command in the South.—A major (his name he does not recollect) is now on his way to recall General Gates,† but purposely delays the business, with a view, to let the old General retrieve his character by some fortunate adventure.—This circumstance,

---

* General Lincoln, who had been taken prisoner in March, when Charleston fell into the hands of the British, was exchanged in November and took part in the campaign.

† On Nov. 13 Gates wrote to Morgan: "I hear by report that I am to be recalled, and that Greene is to succeed to the command of the Southern department. But of this I have not the smallest intimation from Congress, which, I conceive, would have been the case, had the business been finally settled. I think exactly as you do in regard to the command, and am impatient for the arrival of General Greene." A few days afterwards the resolution of Congress superceding Gates arrived, and was followed by the new Commander himself.—Graham's *Morgan.*

from the opinion you have conceived of his *Successor*,* will I am afraid render your Command less agreeable, than it otherwise would have been. If it would not be troublesome, I should be happy to maintian a regular correspondence with you, and if you please, it shall be a confidential one.—Assure Howard & Brooks of my Esteem, and that I will shortly write to them—and make my compliments to every officer under your command.

Yours affectionately
BRYᴺ. BRUIN.

SMALLWOOD TO MORGAN.

CAMP, 6th November, 1780.

Dear Sir:

I have just recᵈ advice from Genˡ Sumter, that a favourable opportunity of effecting something to our advantage offers on the other side the Catawba; you will therefore view the expediency of dispatching your tour below as soon as possible that we may avail ourselves.———We have had no news since

---

* The relations between Morgan and Gates were confidential, but there is nothing beyond the allusion in this letter to show that Morgan entertained any but favorable opinions of Greene. If he suspected him of incapacity before he took command of the Southern Department, he certainly changed his opinion of him before the campaign was over. See Graham's *Morgan* and also T. B. Myers' account of the Battle of Cowpens, containing original letters of Greene and Morgan, printed in the Charleston *News and Courier* in 1881.

you left us, neither of the British in Virginia nor of Gen! Gates's coming on or forwarding the Continental Troops. I expect the Augusta Rifle men here to-morrow, one Hundred and Six in number, these I shall detain here unless you should require them below, as I imagine their service with you at this time will not be wanting—

I am with Sincere regard
Your obd. Hble Serv!
W. SMALLWOOD.

P. S. The Enemy are still in Winsborough, Sumter informs me are likely to remain there for some time—and continue to make *detachments* some distance from their camp—after Provisions & Plunder.

General Morgan.

SMALLWOOD TO MORGAN.

CAMP N. PROVIDENCE, 7th Nov. 1780.

Dear Sir:

I have just rec^d an intimation to be depended on that Tarleton's Legion to the amount of five hundred Cavalry and Infantry mounted, was three days ago at the ferry opposite Camden;* this hint

---

* "The light troops, however, on their arrival at Camden, found no reason to expect an attack from General Morgan, and Lieutenant Colonel Tarleton thought the opportunity favorable to commence an expedition against Marion." Tarleton's *Campaigns*, p. 171.

I think necessary to give, to guard you against a surprise, or any excursion they may have in view to attack you in a divided state, or intercept any of your parties—you will therefore avail yourself of the Hint, and keep a watchful eye on their motions, should they approach upward

I am

with great regard

your ob Hle servt

W. SMALLWOOD.

N. B. (This information comes from Genl Sumpter)——Since writing the above I have it from good authority that Tarleton had crossed to Camden and had moved from there before Day. On Sunday morning, he gave out he was going up the Hanging Rock road, but I rather think he took the road to the High Hills of Santee against Marion, otherwise you must have fallen in with him; he is Four Hundred Strong. I would therefore recommend that you move up & draw your and the principal part of Davies force to a point, covering such detachments as it may be necessary to make; by this means you will be more than sufficient to cope with him should be approach upwards. I shall send a detachment down to join you in the morning, and could wish our force would admit of a strong one. Give me the earliest intimation of occurrences, and your opinion of moving a larger force to you. I am persuaded you will be

vigilant and cautious and then you will have nothing to dread.   Adieu.
    Genl. Morgan.

GENL. GATES TO MORGAN.*

CHARLOTTE, 28th November, 1780.

Dear Sir:

If General Smallwood, General Davidson, and
Colonel Washington, are in opinion with you, it is
a proper time to make an excursion to the Wax-
haws ; I have no Objection to that measure taking
place immediately : but if Lord Cornwallis has
join'd his whole force at Camden—I think it wise
in us to do the same here.

I am
Your affectionate
humble Servant
HORATIO GATES.

Brig. Gen! Morgan.

GATES TO MORGAN.

COL. SMITHS, 15 June, 1781.†

Dear General :

This morning I was acquainted in Winchester

---

* This was one of the last of Gates' orders.   Four days later
Greene took command at Charlotte.

† Gates no longer held any military command.   He was not
restored to his rank until 1783, after all fighting was over.

that you had an Express last Night by the Bearer, Cap^n Reid of State Cavalry, arrived last Night from Staunton. He reports that Baron Steuben had suddenly retreated from the Forks of James River, to Hallifax Court House, on the Back of North Carolina, and that a Quantity of cloathing, & other stores, had been destroyed by the enemy at the forks, which, the Baron had not removed: I suppose, from want of the means. Cap^n Reid futher says, that General Nelson is appointed Governor, in the room of Governor Jefferson—Cap^n Reid further declares, that the Marquis & Lord Cornwallis are only 25 miles asunder, &, that an action between them was daily expected! I confess myself very Anxious for the success of our Army, as the Defeat of the Marquis must at this critical moment be attended with-very serious consequences. I wish I could communicate my thoughts upon the present position of affairs to you this evening as I must return home to-morrow morning early!—perhaps you may be inclined to return here with the Bearer—My best respects wait upon Mrs. Morgan & the Young Ladies.

With much regard I am

Your affectionate

Humble servant

HORATIO GATES.

STEUBEN TO MORGAN.*

NEAR CHARLOTTESVILLE, July, 16, 1781.

Sir:

Col White has just handed me your letter of the 12th Inst.

You must certainly Sir have misunderstood the Marquis, as he knows that I am here for the recovery of my Health & not for the purpose of equipping the Cavalry. Major Call has the superintendence of that business & to him I have refer'd Col White

I am Sir

Your very hum

Servt

STEUBEN

Maj. Genl.

---

*The Battle of the Cowpens had been won Jany. 17th, and after taking his troops to Guilford Court House, Morgan was obliged from bad health to retire from the field. Early in February he went to Fredericksburg, and reached his home in March in great suffering. In May he had recovered sufficiently for active duty, and the Virginia House of Delegates, June 2, 1781, called for his assistance, "to take the command of such Volunteers, Militia, or others, as he may be able speedily to Embody, and march to join the army of the Honorable Major General Marquis de Lafayette." He immediately took measures to raise a large force of militia, but his success, at first, was not encouraging. (Graham's *Morgan.*) His application to Baron Steuben was ill-timed, as Steuben had retired to a friend's country place near Charlottesville, sick and disgusted, and did not take an active part in the campaign until September. (See Kapp's *Life of Steuben.*)

LAFAYETTE TO MORGAN.

MALVERN HILL, 21st July, 1781.*

My dear Sir:

I am very sorry my letter to you Has Been so much delayed—not that any inconvenience Has attended this neglect; But Because I fear future ones which may Be very Hurtful to the Service—However my letters Had been put into the Governor's Hands who promised it should Be sent on immediately.

General Wayne will, no doubt, communicate to you a Letter from me—if His position affords Refreshment, subsistence and security He Had Better Remain there and you with Him—Two or three days will determine what the enemy intend to do, and the distribution of their forces must of course decide what will Become of ours.

In every case you will shortly Rejoin this Army, and I wish you may find on your arrival the expected Reinforcement—it will I think Be well to send them some orders to Hurry their march to camp.

Should you not find any position where you might fight to advantage the Mounted part of the British Army, or should you fear to Be unacquainted with their movements, it would of course

---

* A few days before this Lafayette had put Morgan in command of all the light troops and cavalry.

Be more prudent to Be on this Side—But in the other cases, independant of my aversion to Useless fatigues I am glad to keep the enemy in suspense and should they move up in consequence of our divided state it will Retard their preparations for the Relief of New York.

With the most Sincere Regard and affection

LAFAYETTE

M. G.

LAFAYETTE TO MORGAN.

MALVERN HILL, 21st July 1781.

Dr. Sir:

I had made out instructions for an officer (which I inclose you) to proceed to the British prisoners, when I received an account of Tarleton's return. As sending them to James Town by the route you proposed is now unnecessary you will give orders for them to cross at the Point of fork, and to proceed by slow and easy marches. Our prisoners have not arrived for whom these are to be exchanged.

I am Dr Sir

Your ob S

LAFAYETTE.

Brig. Gen. Morgan.

GOVERNOR NELSON* TO ——————

CAMP BEFORE YORK, 16th Oct 1781.

Sir:

I received your Letter yesterday and am sorry that Major Massie purchased that Horse for General Morgan, because I know he will not suit him. He was once mine. I found him vicious, dull, and that he would stumble, so much as to make it dangerous to ride him; in short, that he had almost every bad quality and not a good one.† If General Morgan chooses to keep him, He must be paid for, but the orders cannot be sent at present.

I am Sir

Your obed servt

THOS. NELSON JR.

BENJ. HARRISON‡ TO MORGAN.

11 Dec , 1781.

Sir:

Your letter§ to Col° Joseph Holmes of the 25th

---

* Thomas Nelson, Jr., had been elected Governor of Virginia June 12, to succeed Thomas Jefferson.

† General Morgan was over six feet high and weighed more than two hundred pounds. General Nelson's solicitude was, therefore, well founded.

‡ Harrison was at this time Speaker of the Virginia House of Burgesses. He was elected Governor in 1752.

§ After the surrender of Cornwallis at Yorktown, "a large proportion of the prisoners surrendered on that occasion were marched to Winchester, and guarded by a body of Militia, were

ult. was by him sent to the executive. It gives me
the greatest concern to hear that the People in your
part of the Country should refuse to part with their
provisions for the purpose of feeding the Guard and
prisoners; I hope before this reaches you the necessity for our impress of those articles will cease,
as the continental and State Commissaries have
enterd into an agreement by which I expect the
former will be enabled to pay for what may be
wanted till he can receive orders on that subject
from Philadelphia, to which place application has
been made for a supply of money; but should none
arrive, and the agreement made by the commissaries fail, recourse must be had to impress till the
first day of January next and no longer, and I must
beg the favor of you to use your influence and assistance on the occasions; whatever may be furnish'd till that time this State will make good as
soon as possible.

The escape of such numbers of the prisoners is
really a matter of moment, and ought to be strictly
inquired into and the negligent punished in the

---

confined in the barracks near that place, under the direction of
Col. Wood, the commissary of prisoners in that section of the
country. The untoward consequences which followed the arrival of these prisoners in Frederick, were the subject of a number of letters from Morgan to Washington, Governor Harrison,
Colonels Wood and Smith, and others in authority." Graham's
Morgan, p. 400. Morgan was then at his home, "Saratoga"
near Winchester, recovering from another attack of illness.

severest manner, will you be so kind as to look into the matter, and so far as is in your power remedy the evil. It will give you some trouble, but I rest assured that will not deter you when you reflect the very great service you will render your country by giving your assistance on the present occasion; I do not mean to press this business on you for any length of time, but will relieve you as soon as possible. As to the riotous officers I dare say you will know how to deal with them, and beg you to act accordingly.

I am with great respect and esteem
Your most obedient and most
Humble servant
BENJ. HARRISON.

BENJ. HARRISON TO MORGAN.

RICHMOND, Decr. 31, 1781.

Sir:

Your favor of the 11th instant came to hand only two days ago; I thank you for your care of the Prisoners of war; and for the measures you have taken to prevent their escaping. That you should not be too much troubled on the occasion, Capt Holmes was appointed to take charge of them, and a letter written to you by him which I suppose has been long since deliver'd. I have hopes from the last informations from Congress that before this reaches you the greater part of these people will be removed out of the State, and that the few which will be left will be furnished by contract, made in Philadelphia.—You will see by the enclosed proclamation that all officers civil and military are order'd to assist in taking up and securing straggling prisoners of war. I hope it will have a good effect as I am determined to punish any person that I can prove has neglected to do his dnty. I am

Your most obedient Humble
Servant
BENJ. HARRISON.

BENJ. HARRISON* TO MORGAN.

RICHᴰ, Feby 23ᵈ, 1782.

Sir:

I am really sorry it is not in my power to comply with your just demands against the country, if it was, you may rest assured the money should be paid, but there is not forty shillings in the Treasury, nor has not been above ten pounds in it, since I have been in the Government, as soon as it is in Cash, which will not be in less than four or five months, you shall be most certainly paid.———

The subject of Claypool† has been already under

---

* He was now Governor of the State.

† In the Spring of 1781, "a party of tories, residing on Lost River, in the then county of Hampshire (now Hardy), had col-

the consideration of the Executive ; they have determin'd that he be bro't down, and I see no reason for an alteration of his term, everything that you urge in his favor having been said before by Rev. Hogg ; the weather is so bad that I cant get a council to-day, when I have one I will again lay the matter before them, and if they should be of opinion that he should be pardon'd I will forward one to you, if you do not receive it very shortly, you may conclude that it will not be granted, and the law must take its course. I do, and ever shall, pay great respect to your recommendations, but in the present case I see so much due to government, that I can not help saying, that clemency in the present instance, at least at this stage of the business, will

---

lected together and raised the British standard. John Claypool, a Scotchman by birth, and his two sons, were at the head of the insurgents.* * * * Claypool had succeeded in drawing over to his party a considerable majority of the people on Lost River, and a number of those on the South Fork of the Wappatomica. * * * * The tories began to organize, they appointed officers, and made John Claypool their colonel, with the intention of marching off in a body to join Cornwallis, in the event of his marching into the valley, or near it." General Morgan assumed command of a force raised against these Tories, captured Claypool and dispersed his adherents. Claypool afterwards expressed great contrition for his conduct and on Feb'y 5, 1782, wrote begging Morgan's interposition in his behalf.—Graham's *Morgan*, p. 378 et seq.

show a want of fortitude in the Governor, and be injurious to the State.

I am,

Sir

Your most ob.^t Hble servt

BENJ HARRISON.

DAVID JAMESON TO MORGAN.

IN CIRCUIT, February 27th, 1782.

Sir:

Claypool having been examined in the county and ordered for Trial at the General court, the Executive have no Right to interfere. Should he be condemned your recommendation of him will have its proper weight in obtaining his pardon.

We are very sorry to inform you there is not a shilling in the Treasury, nor is it probable there will be, till the Taxes are collected under the Revenue act passed last Session of Assembly. Mr Beale presented an Account for clothing &c., furnished some volunteers, and was then told it must be laid before the Assembly. The Executive have in no instance furnished either Clothing for Volunteers or equipments for the Horses—except caps, Swords and Pistols on Loan.

Mr. Campbells account is returned, if the Court

of claims for the County will not admit it, he must apply to the auditors.

   I am Sir

     Your most obedient humble servant

          DAVID JAMESON.

Genl. Morgan.

B. LINCOLN* TO MORGAN.

       WAR OFFICE, Sep! 17th, 1782.

Sir:

  I have been honored with your favor of the 17th instant.

  I am very sorry that it is not in my power to forward you the medal ordered by Congress †—

---

 * He was then Secretary of War.

 † Congress had ordered a gold medal struck for Morgan in appreciation of his conduct at the battle of the Cowpens, but he did not receive it until 1790. It was transmitted to him by Washington, as the following letter shows:

       "NEW YORK, March 25th, 1790.

 "*Sir:* You will receive with this a medal, struck by order of the late Congress, in commemoration of your much approved conduct in the battle of the Cowpens, and presented to you as a mark of the high sense which your country entertains of your services on that occasion.

 "This medal was put into my hands by Mr. Jefferson, and it is with singular pleasure that I now transmit it to you.

      "I am, sir, &c.,

       "GEORGE WASHINGTON.

"Gen. Morgan."

       —Graham's *Morgan*, p. 414.

such are the pressing demands on the finances to feed the army that little money can be supplied for any other purpose. The moment the money can be had I will cause it to be made and forwarded. I am with real esteem regard

Your ob sv^t

B. LINCOLN,

Genl Morgan.

TH. JEFFERSON TO MORGAN NEVILLE, ESQR.*

MONTICELLO, Dec. 18, 19.

Sir :

On receipt of your letter of the 19th I turned to my papers respecting the medals given by Congress to certain officers. They charged their minister of finance with procuring them, and he put the execution into the hands of Col^o Humphreys when he went to Paris as Secretary of legation, but he returned before much progress was made, left the completion with me. I had them compleated and when I returned from France in 1789 I brought two compleat sets, and delivered them to General Washington, the one in silver for himself,

---

* General Morgan's eldest daughter married General Presley Neville, of the Revolutionary army. This letter is to their son. To General Presley Neville the reader will find further allusion in the letters of Gen. La Fayette, and he played an important part in the "Whiskey Insurrection."

the others in gold or silver as voted by Congress was for the officers and delivered to G! Washington to be presented. That to G! Morgan was of gold— each die cost 2400^f and the gold for the medal was 400^f , as an additional charge. Congress had directed copies in silver to be presented to the different sovereigns of Europe and to the Universities of that quarter of our own, this part of the buiness being unfinished and left with Mr. Short and finally I believe dropt. The dies were directed to be deposited in the office of Mr. Grand, banker of the U. S. and I think they were afterwards directed to be sent here and deposited in the treasury office: but of this I am not sure; if they are not in our Treasury they ought still to be in the office of Mr. Grand. The dies were considered as the property of the U. S., and if not sent here, can, I imagine, be found by our minister at Paris, altho' Mr. Grand be dead long since. A Mr. Gautier succeeded in his house, but retired long since to Geneva, is still living as far as I know, and can give information on the subject ; perhaps Mr. Short of Philad' can also give some information. This is the sum of my knowledge of the matter, which is tendered with the assurance of my respect.

TH. JEFFERSON.

Mr. Neville.

CHARLES MAGILL TO MORGAN.

13th June 1796.

Dear General:

When I last had the pleasure of seeing you at Saratoga you kindly observed that when you return'd from Alexᵃ (to which place you shortly meditated a visit) you would adjust the balance of Glassels claim against you as security for Lewis & a small pecuniary matter between us. At that time I did not foresee a circumstance that has lately turn'd up to wit the purchase by M. Norton of M. P. Murrays land from that gentleman & as M. N. & myself have some amounts to adjust that authorizes a requisition for some money from me I hope you will excuse me for requesting that you will direct any of your correspondents in Alexᵃ to pay to Mʳ Murray or order Ten Guineas which I can safely assure you is within the amount of the claims above referr'd to.

Your obedᵗ Serv.

CHAS MAGILL.

Genˡ Morgan.

MORGAN TO ALEXANDER HAMILTON. *

(No DATE, BUT EVIDENTLY 1799.)

Dear Gen!

I have rec^d yours should have answered it sooner but am laboring under a severe Illness, which hath afflicted me some time—

I inclose you an arrangement to assist you in your recruiting Instructions, agreable to your request—

The state of Virg^a is laid off into four divisions of Militia by law, I have regulated the principal districts by them, and the subdistricts and Rendezvouses according to my Ideas of the business in one division or district having the smallest Population; you will observe only four subdistricts, in another, the largest, six—

I am Dr Sir with Sentiments of real friendship & Esteem

Y^r Ob^t & humble Se^vt

DANIEL MORGAN.

Major General Alexander Hamilton.

---

* Morgan had been elected to Congress in 1797, and, after retiring in ill health, was named in connection with a command, in the event of a war with France, which then seemed more than probable. Under date of May 10, 1799, Washington had consulted him in reference to the military measures to be followed in Virginia. It was in connection with these matters that the letter to Hamilton was written.

COLONEL JOHN FRANCIS MERCER.

LIEUT. COL. JOHN F. MERCER TO COL. SIMMS.*

To Colo. Simms:

As you have repeated your request to be furnished by me with some military details of the campaign of 1781, in Virginia, I have hastily thrown together what I can now recollect, in doing which the circumstances which relate personally to myself have been furnish'd, principally because

---

* The date of the letter is not found on the MS., but from the fact that an allusion is made to "President" Madison, and that Mercer died in 1821, it is fair to presume that it was written between 1809 and 1817, during the closing years of Mercer's life.

John Francis Mercer was born in Stafford Co., Va., May 17, 1759, and died in Philadelphia Aug. 30, 1821. He entered the 3ᵈ Virginia Regt. in 1776. His subsequent military career is stated in his narrative. After the surrender at Yorktown he returned to the study of the law, and was from 1782 to 1785 a delegate in Congress. In 1785 he married Sophie, daughter of Richard Sprigg, of West River, Md., and moved soon afterwards to Cedar Creek, Md., his wife's estate, where he resided from that time. He was a delegate to the convention that formed the Constitution of the United States, but disapproved of the plan that was adopted, and refused to sign the document. He was subsequently a member of the legislature and governor of Maryland. He was an anti-federalist in politics, a friend and follower of Thomas Jefferson.

they have been requested, & also because on some occasions many of them have been misrepresented. I have felt a delicacy when I have differ'd from the relations both of Judge Marshall* & Gen'l Tarleton † of the affairs at Green Spring & before Gloucester, but the only proper object of this relation is to exhibit with truth the impressions of the writer.

You ask me what rank I bore, & how, & when I quitted the continental army? I became a captain in the third reg't of the Virginia line from the battle of Brandywine, my commission bearing date from that day. In March 1778 I was appoint'd in gen'l orders at Valley Forge Aid de camp to Maj. Gen'l Lee & in that capacity serv'd at the action at Monmouth courthouse, & afterwards gave my evidence on his trial, which will be found entirely exculpatory of his conduct in that much misunderstood & misrepresented affair.‡ After the sentence of the Court Marshal, suspending Gen'l Lee from all command for one twelve month, was confirm'd by Congress, I determined to quit the army & study law, & in the fall of 1779 I fix'd myself for this purpose at Williamsburg under the

---

*Marshall's *Life of Washington*.

† *A History of the Campaigns of 1780 and 1781 in the Southern Provinces of North America.* By Lieut. Colonel Tarleton.

‡ *Trial of Major General Charles Lee*, p. 116.

auspices & direction of Mr. Jefferson, then lately
appointed Gov'r of Virginia.

At this time the important supplies which Virginia still continued to furnish the armies of the
North & South had attracted the serious attention
of the enemy & it was conceived that she was peculiarly vulnerable at home, from the many large
navigable rivers, rendering the heart of the country at all times easily accessible to a small invading
force, who wou'd risque but little whilst they
could command the waters. In conformity with
this view Gen'ls Matthews & Leslie had successively landed at Portsmouth in the fall of 1780 &
the Legislature of the State were so fully appriz'd
of the designs of the enemy, that they had vested
ample powers in the executive to provide for its
defence, during their recess. Among the earliest
measures adopted by the Executive & which continued afterwards during subsequent invasions, became one of the principal causes of repelling the
enemy & ultimately deciding the war by the catastrophe at Yorktown, was placing the Militia
when call'd into service under the direction of Continental officers, who had been long in service
many of whom were retir'd, having resigned or
become derang'd under an act of Congress, made
in consequence of the reduced number of privates
in the several corps. In conformity to this plan
Gen'l Robert Lawson who had commanded the

fourth Virg'a reg't in the northern army & who
afterwards serv'd with great distinction, as a Brig.
Gen. of Militia at the battle of Guilford courthouse
in North Carolina, on the first intelligence of the
invasion by Leslie received authority by direction
from the Executives at Richmond (to which place
the seat of Government had been remov'd in the
spring of 1780) to raise a legionary corps, to be
compos'd of two reg't of foot, & 1 of horse, to be
form'd of volunteer militia, & to be commanded
by Officers of his own selection & appointment;
who were empower'd to recruit from all corps of
Militia that were draughted into service. It was
in virtue of this authority that I received my first
appointment of Lieut. Col. from Genl. Lawson,
dated the twenty fourth of October, in one of the
reg't of foot, of which the command was given to
Col. James Monroe in a similar manner, & proceeding immediately to collect & organize the
corps in the vicinity of Richmond, we were enabled
in 7 days to cross James River at Westover on the
first of Novr. with about 300 officers & privates &
on the 7th joined a corps of about 1600 men almost
wholly militia & commanded by Genl. Muhlenberg stationed at Everitts,* in front of Smith field.
Before any operations had been commenced, the
advanc'd post of the Enemy about 8 miles dis-

* Everitt's Mills.

tant from Everitts was called in, & about the 20th Gen'l Leslie embark'd his troops & proceeded to join Lord Cornwallis by water. The camp of Gen'l Muhlenberg broke up & the legionary corps, part of which particularly the horse under Col. Bannister were rapidly organizing at Petersburg, were perhaps too precipitately disbanded.

Early in the spring of 1781 Arnold invaded the state & seiz'd on its defenceless capital, but retreating thence toward Portsmouth he plac'd himself in such a situation that Gen'l Washington conceiv'd it practicable by a rapid movement by light troops from the army under his command, combined with a coöperating French naval force, to capture the body of the Enemy. The Marquis De La Fayette was detach'd with 1200 light troops dispos'd in 3 battalions with (I believe) 6 pieces, but had scarcely reach'd the waters of the Chesapeake when the arrival of a reinforcement to Arnold under Gen'l Philips render'd the object impracticable, & he was countermanded. At this crisis however, the junction of Lord Cornwallis with the corps of Arnold & Philips at Petersburg by a rapid march thro' the interior of North Carolina, indicated a combin'd movement of the enemy against Virg'a on so extended a scale as to render the assistance of a body of continental troops essential to the protection of that important & deserving State. The Marquis was therefore again order'd to proceed & the Pennsylvania line under Gen'l Wayne which had lately mutinied & had been destined to join the southern army after the mutiny subsided, was directed to reinforce him in the first instance. At the moment of the arrival of Lord Cornwallis, died Gen'l Philips, & the delay occasion'd by this circumstance had enabled the Marquis to collect unmolested a considerable force of militia on the north side of James river, who were arranged into brigades under the command of continental officers, with three detach'd corps of about 250 men each of select marksmen plac'd under the command of Maj. Call, Dick & Willis* of Virg'a; the field officers of the militia who express'd discontent at having officers associated with & placed over them, were permitted to go home, a permission not acceptable to many of the men & the men who cou'd not but have more confidence in officers of experience, were in general pleased with the arrangement.

The moment however that a combin'd force cou'd operate against the Marquis, it was evident, that a retreat on his part was unavoidable; the separate detachments of Arnold, Philips, & Lord Cornwallis when united consisted of not less than 8000 effective men, of which from 1000 to 1200 were cavalry & mounted infantry. The whole force of

---

* Richard Call, Charles Dick and Francis Willis, Jr.

the Marquis did not exceed about 1000 effective
Cont'l Light Infantry, & about 3000 militia, at
this time commanded by Gen'l Nelson—combin'd
with these might be estimated at most about 200
Contl troops & newly rais'd 18 months men, &
from 6 to 7 hundred militia, then acting under the
orders of Baron Steuben, to protect the stores at
the Point of fork. The militia in both these corps
were fluctuating; as the times of service of some
expir'd, others arriv'd to take their places, but the
above may be fairly consider'd as a medium estimate of that force, previous to the retrograde
movement of the British army. Lord Cornwallis
having cross'd James River below, moved rapidly
on the Marquis at Richmond. The Marquis abandon'd Richmond on his approach, cross'd the
Pamunkey & retreated thro' Hanover on the main
road to Fredericksburg. Lord Cornwallis pursued
him into Hanover county, crossing the Pamunkey
at Bottoms Bridge, & here his sudden halt sacrificed
ev'ry rational object of the campaign. Of these
there were two, but which an intelligent & diligent
officer wou'd necessarily have combin'd. The first
was the army of the Marquis, the destruction of
which (as it contained the only germ of defence)
might have prov'd fatal—by pressing on the right
flank of this corps he must have either overtaken
& destroyed it, or forc'd it below the falls of the
Rappahannock, & by that means involving it be-

tween the Patomack & Rappahannock, or the Rappahannock & Mattapony it must have surrendered
or dispers'd. The practicability of this operation
must be evident to who ever reflects that he had
the command of from 1000 to 1200 cavalry &
mounted infantry, a number superior to the whole
Cont'l force in the Marquis's army, & the main
bodies of the two Armies were not twenty miles
distant, when the halt was made at Bottom's bridge.
The Marquis at this time had not more than 50
Dragoons, the remnant of Armands corps, & 15 or
20 volunteer cavalry, under Capt. Page—these were
not only in number entirely inadequate to performing reconoitring duty, but were worn down with
incessant fatigue. It was therefore utterly impossible for the Marquis to escape, if diligently watch'd
& harrass'd by so formidable a corps of horse.
This was plainly seen the day after the British
army cross'd the bridge, the Army of the Marquis
was compell'd to halt and stand to their arms by
the sudden appearance of Tarleton, who after this
unmeaning bravado, retir'd to the main body. It
was unnecessary for him to risque anything, the
Marquis dare not march in his presence & Thus
retarded, Lord Cornwallis must necessarily have
brought him to action & the event cou'd not be
doubtful.* There was one other important object

* "At this period, the superiority of the [British] army, and
the great superiority of the light troops, were such as to have

of the campaign, which might have been combin'd
with the destruction of the Marquis's corps, this
was the occupation of Fredericksburg & Falmouth
or rather the heights above the latter. The importance of this position had been well understood by
Gen. Philips, the ignorance of Lord Cornwallis
might explain but not excuse his error. A manufactory of small arms had been established at Fredericksburg at the commencement of the revolution,
& connected with similar & more extensive establishments at Hunters Forge above Falmouth on
the opposite side of the river, constituted the most
valuable manufactory of arms & military equipments in the southern states—added to this, these
places were rich depots of Tobacco, & Fredericksburg at that time was the most flourishing town in
the State; but these were not the most essential objects, as a position this was by far the most important in Virg'a, the wide navigable waters of the Patomack approach the Rappahannock here within
seven miles, beyond which there navigable for
frigates near 60 miles, on the flank & rear of the
position, to Alexandria & Georgetown—at Boyds
hole the station for a fleet of the largest ships is as

---

enabled the British to traverse the country without apprehension or difficulty, either to destroy stores and tobacco in the
neighborhood of the rivers, or to undertake more important
expeditions." Tarleton's *Campaigns, p. 294.*

safe & capacious as the harbours of Yorktown & Portsmouth & would be completely cover'd by an army posted on the hills above the falls, on the north side of the Rappahannock, with which there wou'd be an open safe water communication except for about 6 or 7 miles constituting a pass so intersected with hills & water courses as to be entirely commanded by an army so posted. This position then commanded the two towns of Fred'g & Falmouth, the main road to the northern states, & the communication with the lower counties, the large and fertile peninsula, inclos'd between the Patomack & Rappahannock abounding in supplies and inhabited by a numerous black population, would be entirely at the mercy of the British army. The larger & equally fertile Peninsula between the Rappahannock & York, & its northern branch the Mattapony from similar population wou'd be almost as incapable of defence. From Fred'g to Charlottesville is about 60 miles, the same as from Richmond; to the northern passes in the Blue Mountains still less. The army of Lord Cornwallis therefore possess'd of this position, connected with their naval force, brought into the Patomack & with so large a body of cavalry that might be encreas'd in this country at will, would command & threaten a great portion of the State, would disconnect the lower country from the back country & the northern states & would cut off the southern

army from all supplies from the northern states &
even communication with the northern army, except by the circuitous & almost impracticable rout
beyond the Blue mountains which [*MS. torn*]
would in fine if it did not effect a conquest of, it
would infallibly paralize all the efforts of Virg'a.

With military men who had reflected on these
combinations there cou'd not remain a doubt but
that Lord Cornwallis, whether he succeeded in his
views against the Marquis or not, wou'd occupy
Frederick'g and Falmouth at least for a time.
Such certainly was my impression, & I resided there
in the beginning of May 1781, having commenced
the practice of the law there the winter before, on
the disbanding of Lawson's corps. At this junc-
ture Gen'l Weedon took the command of about 5
hundred militia, collected to cover this position &
as the towns of Fredericksburg & Falmouth are
commanded by the surrounding heights, he aban-
doned them withdrawing whatever might be an
object to the enemy & took an advantageous post
on the heights above Hunters works, in order to
protect them from the insult of an inferior detachment. It was here that Gen'l Weedon communicated to me a letter from the Marquis de la Fayette
stating his total want of & great distress for cavalry,
& conveying a request that I would exert myself
to raise a volunteer corps of horse. With the assistance of Mr. Washington the present judge, then

a youth of twenty, Mr. Ludwell Lee, the Mr. Brents, & other young gentlemen a corps was collected, arm'd and march'd in less than a week. At first it did not exceed 30, it gradually however grew in numbers & reputation, but never exceeded 50 on duty at any one time; they furnish'd their horses & arms themselves & paid their own expences until all their resourses were exhausted, without recurring to the distressing modes which the decline of paper money had render'd almost indispensable & universal, requisition, impressment & payment in certificates. This troop join'd the Marquis in Hanover county, at the moment that Col. Tarleton had made the demonstration before related, whilst the American troops were drawn up expecting an immediate attack; & were instrumental in ascertaining that the enemy in view were only a reconnoitring party. The moment they dispearred the Marquis abandon'd the road to Fred. & leaving that position to its fate, directed his march thro' the upper part of Spotsylvania & cross'd the head waters of Mattapony in the route to Orange courthouse with the view of forming a junction with Wayne & gaining the upper country thro' which Wayne was then marching.

The delay at Bottoms bridge decided the fate of this campaign. The destruction of the Marquis's corps & the position at Frederick were relinquished in favor of a Quixottic expedition against the members of the legislature at Charlottesville,* who with great facility mov'd their quarters & who had they been taken cou'd only have prov'd an incumbrance & another as trifling, which terminated in the destruction of a few rusty musquits as the point of fear. To favour these two operations the main body of the British Army mov'd to their left into Goochland county, & the Marquis de la Fayette having effected a junction with Wayne, mov'd rapidly across the country to James River, in order to cover the stores at Albemarle court house & being now also reinforced by a considerable body of Militia, he deem'd his force sufficient to watch the movements of the enemy & to prevent their operations by detachments. Before this last movement Gen. Nelson being elected Gov'r of Vir'a left the army to qualify & to attend to other duties of the office & did not join it again until it had taken post at W'msburg some short time before the siege of York. Early in June, Lord Cornwallis fell back upon Richmond, & the Marquis de la Fayette fix'd his headquarters at Dandridge about 20 miles above. The armies lay 8 or 10 days in these positions inactive, except that an attempt was made by Col. Tarleton to strike at the corps of Muhlenberg, but without success, after

---

* " . . . To distress the Americans, by breaking up the assembly at Charlottesville."—*Tarleton, p. 295. See Letters of Joseph Jones,* p. 82.

this the enemy evacuated Richmond & mov'd on
slowly to W'msberg by new Kent court house, his
rear protected by the legions of Tarleton & Simcoe.
The Marquis follow'd him cautiously at an interval of from 20 to 30 miles & arriv'd at what was
called Mr. Frye's plantation (formerly Duncastle's
ordinary) 16 miles from Williamsburg on the main
road to Fred'g by Ruffins ferry, having plann'd &
executed an attack on Simcoe's corps which had not
yet entered Williamsburg. The command of this
enterprize was given to Col. Butler* assisted by the
Dragoons of Armand, under Maj. McPherson. I
was not present but I then collected from several
officers that were (some of whom were taken prisoners in that action,) that Col. Simcoe was completely surpriz'd at Hot Water near 7 miles above
W'msburg;† the rifle men of Call & Willis of Virg'a
made the attack & drove the Hessian Jagers upon
the Infantry of the legion, who being also fir'd on,
whilst they were forming, began to give way,
when a Lieutenant Lollar ‡ of the horse of Simcoe,
at the head of not more than 50 dragoons, hastily
collected, made a well timed & furious charge first
on the Dragoons of Armand & having overturn'd

---

* Percival Butler, of Pennsylvania.

† The place is better known as Spencer's ordinary. I find no
other writer describing it as Hot Water.

‡ It was Captain Shank who commanded in this charge.

them, wounding and taking prisoners Lieut. Brife*
& some privates of that corps, charg'd thro' the
rifle men, who were at that time passing a lane in
pursuit. These fled precipitately & dispersed,
whilst the Continental infantry remained in order
at a distance & never fir'd a gun; they however
protected the retreat of the militia, which became
soon necessary, as Lord Cornwallis arriv'd on the
ground within less than an hour after the fighting
began with his best troops—on his arrival at the
head of his line he was address'd by Col. Simcoe
with information at his success, but replied (as I
was inform'd by an officer who was then a prisoner
& heard the conversation) with the reproachful ob-
servation that no officer ever receiv'd a surprize.
Col. Simcoe had never been a favorite, he appears to
have declin'd in activity and health after this morti-
fying repulse, & he seem'd by no means recover'd,
when his legion surrender'd at Gloucester.†

From the time that my volunteer corps had
join'd the Marquis their activity & good conduct
had distinguish'd them in the army, where such
corps had before fallen into disrepute; the duty they

---

* Dr. Egle gives a roster of Armand's legion, and in the sixth
corps the lieutenant was Augustin Briffault—the only name that
is at all like Brife.

† This does not agree with Col. Tarleton's account. See
Tarleton's *Campaigns*, p 301 ; Clinton-Cornwallis Controversy,
II., 32 ; Simcoe, *Journal*, 235; Lossing, *Field Book*, II., 258.

had perform'd wou'd have destroy'd the same
number of any regular troop: their youth, their
spirit & the honourable pride incident to their station in life, encourag'd them to attempt any thing,
and accustom'd to ride in the woods their fine
horses extricated them when surrounded by the
numerous adverse cavalry; they liv'd on the flanks
& rear of the enemy, and altho' few days pass'd
without some of them & often the whole corps being pursued by parties greatly superior in number,
yet they sustained no loss themselves, on the contrary the day Tarleton made the movement against
Muhlenberg, they proceeded to Richmond, alarm'd
the Pickett on Shockhoe hill, fell into Tarleton's
rear, carried off his Parolle & conducted them safe
thro' the woods to the American camp, altho' the
whole force of Tarleton was then in motion between.   These were the only prisoners made by
any part of the army during the summer campaign
that I recollect, certainly they were the only horsemen that were taken.   The troops enter'd Richmond as the enemy quitted it, & whilst the enemy
lay at W'msburg the Marquis having information
that Lord Cornwallis was on the eve of crossing the
James river, directed this corps to obtain the earliest intelligence of the movement; for this purpose
they made a circuitous march of twenty miles &
halted in a skirt of wood back of the Palace during
the night, & were at Lord Cornwallis's head

quarters (President Madison's at Wm. and Mary college*) a very short time after he left them, & appriz'd the Marquis of his movements & designs in time for him to put his troops in motion that evening. The American army halted that night about 8 or 10 miles from the enemy, & early in the morning of the 6th of July I rode up to Green Spring house & was informed by a Black with a knapsack at his back standing at the door, that it was the quarters of Col. Tarleton who (he said) was then in a spring house a few yds. distant; during the conversation myself & three or four young gentlemen with me, found ourselves suddenly surrounded in a decay'd yard formed of brick walls, but the enemy by pushing to cut off our retreat enabled us to escape in a contrary direction, & out riding them in the wood I was enabled to regain my troop, which I had placed in cover on the road. The manner in which I had gain'd this intelligence which was so abrupt as to admit of no deception, & what I saw of the enemys force, satisfied me that their main Body had not cross'd & was not crossing, & I gave this as my decided opinion to the Marquis at 11 o'clock, whilst advancing with his troops. Previous to this he had dispatch'd two Gent'e of my corps Mr. Washington & Mr. Lee with his glasses to reconnoitre the ferry, & unaccustomed to the appearance of armies, they were de-

* Rev. James Madison was then President of the college.

ceiv'd by the passage of the Queens Rangers & the numerous followers of the army, into a persuasion that the main body had crossed.

THE ACTION OF GREEN SPRING.

At one o'clock the Marquis & Gen'l Wayne with their parties arrived at Green Spring house, which now exhibited no appearance of an enemy, & receiving this, and other intelligence, the confidence of Gen'l Wayne that we had only a covering party in front prevailed, & it was determined to hazard an action, in the attempt to cut them off. The ground in front of the house at Green Spring was most unfavorable for such an enterprize, a morass & wood protected & cover'd the front of the enemy, & presented no approach but by a causeway of considerable extent forming part of the main road leading to the Church, which render'd even reconnoitring with effect unsafe, unless protected by a strong body of troops, & such a corps when beyond the ravine were expos'd to eminent risque; a few scattering volunteers on horseback pass'd the causeway, & were soon follow'd by about 300 riflemen, who enter'd the wood at three o'clock with great caution. At 4 the main body of the Continental troops took up their line of march, the riflemen who had advanc'd were divided into two corps on the right & left of the road of a hundred & fifty men each, to protect the flanks. Maj. McPherson and the head

of Armand's horse led the column, I follow'd with
my troops, then at a considerable interval the Continental light infantry were followed by Gen'l
Wayne's brigade, the whole amounting to 2200
effective men, a force rather unequal to 8000, the
flower of the British army, posted with ev'ry advantage not now more that a mile in front. The
militia were directed to form as a reserve, back of
Green Spring house. The column had scarcely
advanced half a mile thro' an open wood, when
some scattering shot & retreating volunteers an-
nounced the vicinity of the enemy. Maj. McPherson, who from the commencement, had form'd just
ideas of the relative situation of the two armies &
consequently no very favorable impression of our
present movements, appriz'd the Gen'l of our nigh
approach, but he immediately received an order
to take command of the 150 Riflemen on the left,
whilst I was ordered to direct the attack on the
right, with a similar number.—400 yards on the
right of the road, where the column halted, I found
the Riflemen advanc'd near the edge of the wood, &
firing at long shot on the sentinels of a Pickett
paraded before a small clapboard house; along
the front of the wood, & and to the left ran a ditch
& post & rail fence to this house; beyond this fence
was an open field in which the horse of Tarleton
were form'd, at the respectable distance of four or
five hundred yards; their left flank was protected

by a skirt of woods, in front of which was form'd a Pickett of 100 or 150 men, beyond this on the right of Tarleton, & across the main road & in front of the church appeared, indistinctly, the main body of the British army. I judged it necessary to attack the Pickett at the house; to advance into the field if the riflemen could be persuaded to risque it, would have expos'd them to the horse, & wou'd have left this Pickett in the flank and rear.—By encouragement & example they were gradually advanc'd obliquely to the left in the ditch & cover'd from the house by the fence & the Pickett was speedily driven with loss, & possession gain'd of the house. To support them & regain the house, the Pickett on the left of Tarleton advanc'd with spirit, but they were unable to stand the deadly fire of the Riflemen, and were driven back with the loss of the officer who led them, who was wounded & taken prisoner with several men; the Riflemen embolden'd by this success, were with difficulty restrain'd from advancing into the open field against the horse & a number of them crowded into the house & began to fire to the left on the main body of the British army now plainly discover'd, at the distance of about 300 yards. At this moment my troops was sent to me; they became consequently much exposed & cou'd be of no possible use; however to encourage the Riflemen, & give them confidence, I drew them up in a lane which led towards the main road & the enemy, & at the same time Maj. Galvan advanc'd along the main road with about 150 light infantry to the front of the wood, form'd to the left of the horse & began to fire at long shot on the enemy's army. The British Gen'l & Staff immediately clear'd their front & open'd 3 pieces of artillery on us, at from three to four hundred yards. Almost at the first discharge my horse received a cannon ball in his body, which carried away my stirrups & bruis'd my foot, several of the troop were dismounted, the shot passing through the clapboard house alarming the Riflemen within so much that they fled instantly with great trepidation; by this time I had mounted another horse, but it was impossible to rally those who had fled or stop those advanced into the field, who dispers'd in great confusion. The whole front line of the enemy was now advancing with shouts. At this moment arriv'd Cap't Savage with two pieces of artillery at the clapboard house, & a Battalion of Cont. light infantry under Maj. Willis of Connecticut. I had no hesitation in advising Capt. Savage to withdraw his artillery as fast as possible as nothing else cou'd prevent their instant capture; he follow'd this advice with reluctance & sav'd his pieces. Maj. Willis retir'd by the right without firing a gun & without any advice & Maj. Galvan after firing some rounds with his 150 men on the British line, now formed &

advancing, was soon compell'd to retreat with precipitation. This advanced corps being entirely dispers'd, the wounded in our possession were retaken by the enemy. I fell back with a few of my troops having order'd on the others to join a party who acted as body guard to the Marquiss. At the distance of about 300 yards in the rear of where we had been engaged, I found Gen'l. Wayne's Brigade drawn up across the road & thro' the wood to the right. I staid with them until they were defeated. We had just begun to assume the stiff German tactics, as the British acquir'd the good sense, from experience in our woody country, to lay it aside.*

Gen'l Wayne's Brigade were drawn up in such close order as to render it utterly impracticable to advance in line & preserve their order—the line was necessarily broke by the trees as they pass'd the wood. The British advanc'd in open order at arm's length & aiming very low kept up a deadly fire. In this situation Gen'l Wayne gave repeated orders for the line to charge, but this operation was really impossible from the manner in which they were form'd & they cou'd not be push'd forward; notwithstanding his own bravery & the ardor of an admirable corps of field officers, who gave them the best examples, the destruction amongst them was very great, whilst the effect of their own fire, from

* A hit at Steuben who was very unpopular in Virginia.

the causes already explain'd, was I believe very
trifling, & I have always retain'd the opinion that
the enemy suffer'd more from the Riflemen on the
right & Galvan's corps, than from all the rest of the
Marquis' troops in this action.—In less than 30
minutes from the retreat of the advanc'd corps, the
rout was total and our flying & dispers'd soldiers
escap'd along the causeway & thro' the morass.
During the whole action the Marquis remain'd
with a few horse a small distance in the rear of
Wayne *—he did nothing and in fact in the situation things were, after the attempt to reinforce the
advanc'd corps, nothing cou'd be done, but to submit to a disgraceful defeat. Fortunately it terminated better than cou'd have been expected, had the
British horse (who never made an effort during the
action, when the brigade of Wayne gave way)
charg'd down the road, & taken possession of
Green Spring, only defended by some frighten'd
militia, very few of the Continental troops cou'd
have escaped, the Marquis's army wou'd have
been broken & dispers'd, & Lord Cornwallis wou'd
have escap'd the catastrophe at York. As it was

---

*This is at variance with the printed accounts. Johnston
(*The Yorktown Campaign and the Surrender of Cornwallis*)
says Wayne's movement "was successful, though costly," and
that Lafayette "exposed himself at the front, when he saw that
Wayne had become engaged," pp. 65, 66. This is substantially
the same as Marshall's brief description—Marshall's *Life of
Washington*, Vol. 4, p. 400 et seq. (Edition of 1805.)

the troops collected that night a few miles beyond Green Spring & the next day being not pursued, & being join'd by an excellent corps of horse from Baltimore commanded by Capt. More & having preserv'd all their baggage, soon forgot the disaster of this day. The British were therefore perfectly right when they speak of defeating the militia in the commencement of this action; they defeated those I commanded, who being reinforced by the corps of Galvan & Willis, the corps of volunteer horse & two pieces of artillery made no doubt a very formidable appearance, altho' none of them did any mischief, except the Riflemen & Galvan's & the latter not much. When our accounts speak nothing of the engagement of the advanc'd militia it only shews that such confusion reign'd that no one had any just knowledge of this affair who has yet describ'd it. Thus terminated one of the most silly & misjudged affairs that took place during the war. There was no good reason to think Lord Cornwallis wou'd risque a covering party & indeed it ought to have been known that James Island where the action was fought affords ample protection to the rear of a crossing army. The Gen'ls never had any good reason to believe the army had crossed & they were furnish'd with proofs to the contrary at ev'ry step; they had it in their power to withdraw the corps they had risqued beyond the causeway at any time before the artillery were ad-

vanc'd with Galvan & Willis;—afterwards it required all the bravery of Wayne & his corps &
above all, the misconduct of the enemy, to save the
whole from capture.* The next day the Marquis
thought proper to compliment my corps highly in
general orders,† which indeed they always de-
served, but on that day none of them were with me
till towards the close of the action of small arms, &
altho' afterward they were expos'd to great danger
they cou'd not possibly render any service.   Many

---

* "The events of this day were particularly important, and
claimed more attention than they obtained. The Marquis de
la Fayette had made a long march in very sultry weather, with
about fifteen hundred continentals and one thousand militia, to
strike at the rear of the British before they passed to James island.   Too great ardour, or false intelligence, which is most
probable, for it is the only instance of this officer committing
himself during a very difficult campaign, prompted him to cross
a morass to attack Earl Cornwallis, who routed him, took his
cannon, and must inevitably have destroyed his army, if night
had not intervened.   His lordship might certainly have derived
more advantage from his victory.   If the two battalions of light
infantry, the guards, and Colonel Yorke's brigade, who had all
been slightly engaged, or any other corps, and the cavalry, had
been detached, without knapsacks, before dawn of day, to pur-
sue the Americans, and push them to the utmost, the army of
the Marquis de la Fayette must have been annihilated. Such
an exploit would have been easy, fortunate, and glorious, and
would have prevented the combination which produced the fall
of Yorktown and Gloucester."—Tarleton's *Campaigns*, p. 355.

† "The zeal of Colonel Mercer's little corps is handsomely
expressed in the number of horses he had killed." Lafayette's
General Orders of July 8th.

of the gentlemen of this corps being dismounted,
& all exhausted & finding that the armies were
about to operate on the south side of James River,
I obtain'd permission for the Corps to return to
their homes & I know nothing farther of the military transactions of this campaign 'till the siege of
York & Gloucester, but believe they were alto-
gether unimportant & almost devoid of military
incidents.

SIEGE OF YORK & GLOUCESTER.

The combin'd American and French army under
Gen'l Washington & Count Rochambeau having
taken their position before York town, & the Count
de Grasse having taken his station at the mouth
of the river with his fleet, the army of Lord Cornwallis became completely invested on the south
side of the river. On the north side, the British
held the small town of Gloucester, defended by the
legions of Simcoe & Tarleton, cavalry & infantry,
a detachment of mounted British light infantry,
& the 80th or Edinburgh volunteers, a very
strong reg't command by Col. Dundass, the whole
consisting of about 2200 effective troops, but to restrain the operation of this body of which a great
proportion were cavalry & who forag'd the country
in ev'ry direction, no effective American force had
been collected as late as the middle of Sept. A
few scattering militia & mounted volunteers under

the comand of Col. John Taylor of Caroline &
who rarely ventured beyond Gloucester Court
House, left the lower part of that country very
much at the discretion of the British. Early in
Sept. Gen'l Weedon being about to take the command of the troops destined to act against Gloucester, applied to me to accompany him, promising
me a command of select militia; I consented &
Gen'l Weedon reliev'd Col. Taylor, who return'd
home after a fatiguing & hazardous tour of duty;
Gen'l Weedon being soon reinforc'd by several
militia detachments from the Upper counties, took
post at Dixons mill about the middle of Sept. &
soon after Brigadier Gen'l Choisy, promoted during
the seige to the rank of Maj. Gen'l, join'd us with
the legion of the Duke de Lauzun, & on the 25th
he was farther reinforc'd by about 1000 marines
from the French fleet. Gen'l Choisy having now
the command of 1600 French regular troops &
about 2000 American militia, deem'd himself
strong enough to commence operations against the
enemy.

Agreeably to Gen'l Weedon's order, I had selected
from the militia such old soldiers as I cou'd find,
who having retir'd from the army after the expira-
tion of their term of service, were now performing
their tours of duty with the militia as other citizens;
to these I added the most likely young men that
volunteer'd their services & such young gentlemen

as officers as appear'd most promising; personally I was acquainted with none of them. Of such materials I collected a corps consisting of 200 rank & file & a proportionate number of officers; without much relation to size, as a distinction that appear'd best calculated to create an esprit du corps, they were termed the Grenadier reg't. After arming & disciplining them in the best manner time & circumstances wou'd permit, they were attach'd to the legion of Lauzun, the infantry of which did not exceed 350 men, fit for duty. *Until this time I had acted without any commission, but the court of my native county of Stafford, probably being appriz'd of the circumstances, recommended me to the Executive, who forwarded me a commission as Lieut. Col. of the militia of that county, but which was not necessary to confer an authority that was never disputed.*

ACTION BEFORE GLOUCESTER.

Early on the morning of the 2nd of Oct. I was order'd with my corps to join Lieut. Col. Count Robert Dillon who with 150 of the Dragoons of Lauzun was directed to gain the road that led to Gloucester by York river & to move on towards that Post: whilst Gen. Choisy & the Duc de Lauzun at the head of 150 Dragoons proceeded down the Severn road in the same direction, follow'd at a considerable interval by the French & American infantry—the whole intended to take up a position as near as practicable to the town of Gloucester. The interval in which the Dragoons mov'd in advance of the French infantry was soon greatly increas'd, when it was found that the legions of Tarleton & Simcoe were out foraging, & by the anxiety of the French Gen'l & officers to fall in with them. At 10 o'clock some scattering fire was heard in front & and an order came to Count Dillon to advance with his horse [MS. torn] that the legions of Tarleton & Simcoe being over-taken by Gen'l Choisy had halted & that as the Gen'l had no infantry with him, he requested me to hasten my march, by dismounting & setting an example to the corps by running; we were not much behind the horse & when we arriv'd within about 3 or four miles of Gloucester, emerging from the wood I found the two roads uniting in a lane in front, of near a mile in extent, a fence on each side enclosing a large open field, on the right & left. On the right were two houses, the first of which we approach'd became afterwards the quarters of Gen'l Weedon, this was contiguous to the lane; the second, at some distance from the lane, became the quarters of Gen'l Choisy. This lane led into an extensive open old field, where the fences dividing to right & left at right angles, seperated the fields on each side from the old field in front. On the left, at the mouth of the lane commenced a wood which running to the left of the main road for more than a mile, terminated in a small advanc'd redoubt, commanding the main road; to the right of this redoubt facing Gloucester appear'd a post & rail fence which running to the right, at right angles with the road, enclos'd the old field in the rear. In this old field the British horse appear'd to be form'd in line, advanc'd of the redoubt. The dragoons under Dillon passing the lane join'd those under Gen'l Choisy & the Duke at the mouth,—& immediately charg'd the right of Tarleton's line, which broke & gave way, but at the same time the French being receiv'd by musquetry from the post & rail fence in the rear of the British horse, & from the wood in their right, found it necessary to fall back—which they did slowly with order & firmness under the fire of the enemy until they found that my corps was just emerging from the mouth of the lane, when the fire of the musquetry being considerably advanc'd in the wood on their right flank, they made a rapid movement & fell behind my corps into the lane, where they fac'd about & their officers ranged themselves in front to receive the charge of the British horse, now form'd again & advancing in a line with their infantry in the wood.

My little corps of raw troops which did not exceed 160 Rank & file fit for duty, were at first some what startled to find the French horse retreating so rapidly by them in the open field expos'd to at

least 460 horse of the enemy & a body of Infantry
in the wood & their situation was evidently render'd more critical by having a very high fence in
their rear & the lane they advanc'd thro' block'd
up by the French horse. However they were immediately order'd to deploy so as to push their left
flank into the wood, which they did with great cel-
erity & good order, & commenced firing, one half
on the cavalry on the right, & the other half on
the infantry advancing rapidly thro' this wood.
The horse of the enemy had approach'd within 250
yards & the infantry were not at more than 150
yards distance, when the firing began. No regular
troops cou'd behave with more zeal & alacrity than
this corps of Militia; their spirits had been rais'd
by running them up, and being hurried into action
without time to reflect on their danger, they dis-
covered as much gallantry & order as any regular
corps that I ever saw in action. Fortunately Tarleton did not like the reception prepared for him &
at a critical moment sounded a retreat, when not
100 cartridges remain'd unexpended in the regiment; the British troop left Lieut. Moir dead on
the field, within 10 paces of our line, & there ended
this action, which Col. Tarleton justly calls a
trifling affair, but when he says he only notices it
as having been so much misrepresented,* I can only

---

* No such statement appears in Tarleton's *Campaigns*.

say that he has not been more fortunate in his relation than those (whoever they were) of whom
he complains. Thus when he says he found the
whole French & American Infantry advanc'd to the
edge of the wood* (if I recollect right, for I quote
from memory) it is a shameful misrepresentation;
there was not one French or American foot soldier
within 2 or perhaps three miles, except this corps
of 160 militia : the infantry of the legion of Lauzun
first arriv'd, with their field pieces, but they were
not on the ground till 30 minutes after the firing
ceased. From the fire this corps kept up, Col.
Tarleton no doubt concluded them much more
numerous than they were—but nothing cou'd excuse his not proving the fact, with his great superiority. That night I took possession of the advanc'd redoubt on the main road, with 150 French
& 150 Americans; & the French & American
troops encamp'd in the fields on each side of the
lane. The siege continued a tiresome, uniterest-
ing blockade on the Gloucester side, without military incidents, except that men were repeatedly &
uselessly sacrificed by the French Gen'l in idle reconnoitring; the day before the surrender & when
the capitulation had been agreed on at York, Col.
Tarleton came out and dined with Gen'l Choisy;

---

* "The French hussars retired behind their infantry and a
numerous militia who had arrived at the edge of the plain."
Tarleton's *Campaigns*, p. 378.

his object seemed to be to represent that his life might be endangered if he surrendered to the militia, & [MS. torn] was so accommodating as to order that no infantry except that of the legion of Lauzun & my corps shou'd be present at the surrender. We march'd for that purpose 2 miles in front of the camp, & after the arms were piled on the outside of the breastworks, Col. Hugo of the legion & myself took possession of a redoubt & thus ended the campaign in Virginia of 1781.

A few days after Gen'l Washington in Gen'l Orders noticed this action* of the 2d & returned

---

* "The General congratulates the Army upon the brilliant success of the allied Troops near Gloucester. He requests the Duke of Lauzun to accept his particular thanks for the judicious disposition and the decisive vigour with which he charged the enemy—and to communicate his warmest acknowledgments to the Gallant officers and men by whom he was so admirably seconded. He feels peculiar satisfaction at the inconsiderable loss on our part, that no ill effects are to be apprehended from the Honorable Wounds which have been received in this affair, and that at so small an expence, the enemy amounting to six hundred Horse and foot were completely repulsed and Reconducted to their very lines.

"The corps of the allied Army were Duke de Lauzun's Legion and the Militia Grenadiers of Mercer.

"The following is the list of our killed and wounded, and as far as can be gathered of the Enemies—the Duke de Lauzun's Legion had three Hussars Killed—Captains Billy Dillon and Dutester with eleven Hussars Wounded (the officers very slightly)—three horses killed and four wounded.

"The enemy's loss in killed and wounded exceeds fifty, in-his thanks to the legion of Lauzun & the Grenadiers of Mercer for their conduct; these terms did not satisfy some of my friends on the Gloucester side, particularly Col. Innes who was next in command to Gen'l Weedon & who found however on enquiry that the gen'l orders in that report were but a transcript of the report of General Choisy.

---

cluding the commanding officer of the Infantry killed, and Colonel Tarlton badly wounded."—From Washington's *General Orders*, Thursday, October 4, 1781.   State Dept. MSS.

GENERAL LAFAYETTE.

LAFAYETTE TO GEORGE AUGUSTINE WASHINGTON. *

ON BOARD THE ALLIANCE,
December 22d, 1781.

I could not think of going, my dear George, Before I send you this last assurance of my sincere affection—My Best wishes attend you, whatever you may Be doing during the winter—I anticipate the pleasure to see you again with me, and Hope the family will be Reunited in the campaign—Be so kind, my dear Washington, to forward the inclosed letters, and to send them by some good opportunity. You will greatly oblige me, my dear friend, to give [me] copies of my letters to the General, as you know I never kept any, and when I grow old I will find great satisfaction in Reading over our Correspondence during the Last Campaign.

There is one other thing that would give me great pleasure—the General has several Orderly Books from the beginning of the War, and there are Orderly Books of mine in the light infantry of the two last campaigns which I would like to Have copied By some Sergeant that writes a fair Hand

---

* General Washington's nephew, who had served as an aid to Lafayette. He died in February, 1793.

(63)

and Bound up in Books in the same way as those of the General are—if that does not give you too much trouble I will be obliged to you to Have the Business done By some non-commissioned officer that can write well.

In your letters to your family, I Beg you will mention me most affectionately to them—particularly your father and mother, Mrs. Ball and the Colonel,* Mrs. Lewis,† Mrs. Carter‡ and the General's mother—My best compliments to Smith§ and all the family—Adieu, my dear friend, most affectionately Yours,

LAFAYETTE,

If Miss Carter is still in Philadelphia present my best Respects to Her.

LAFAYETTE TO MADAME JULLIEN.

LA GRANGE, 9 Octobre, 1814.

J'avais pensé, Madame, que votre fils Reviendrait á paris pour L'épogue des élections: il se proposait même de donner quelque extension à son manuel des élections et je crois pour cet objet qu'il

---

* Col. Burges Ball and his wife, Frances Washington Ball. She was a daughter of Charles Washington, own brother of the General.

† Betty Lewis, wife of Fielding Lewis.

‡ Wife of Charles Carter, and daughter of Fielding Lewis.

§ William S. Smith.

m'avait emprunté un ouvrage anglais en deux vol-
umes intitulé History of the Borough of Great
Britain. Cet auvrage a été confié par lui à un
citoien des etats unis qui devait coopérer à son tra-
vail. Voilà les élections terminées; je ne sais quand
votre fils m'attendra, et je prends la liberté de
m'adresser à vous, madame, pour avoir de ses nouvelles et des nouvelles de mon Histoire des Bourgs
Britannique. Je vous prie d'avoir la Bonté de me
la faire parvenir si elle est à paris, car je pense
qu'on en a tire ce qui pourra Remplir l'objet des
collaborations. C'est avec plaisir que je profite de
cette occasion pour une Rappellerà vos Bontés et
pour vous offrir l'expression de mon respectueux
attachement.

LAFAYETTE.

LAFAYETTE TO MONROE. *

PARIS, May 10th 1824.

Sir:

The high favor Conferred upon me By the Repre-
sentatives of the people of the United States, the
testimonies of public Benevolence Contained in
their resolution Have filled my Heart with feelings

---

* On Feb'y 7, 1824, President Monroe wrote Lafayette informing him of the wish of Congress that he should visit America.
He enclosed the Congressional resolutions. Under date of April,
1824, Lafayette replied, and subsequently sent the letter of
May 10th given above.

of Respectful, affectionate and patriotic gratitude which I want adequate words to express. No answer can I find more Congenial to these feelings than to embark as soon as possible for the Blessed Shore, I Have for so many years longed to Review. Nor can I fear, impressed as I am with a proud sense of the Honor to Be on Board a National ship, therein will appear irreverence on my part when I Beg leave not to avail my self of the flattering Offer which, in their extreme kindness Congress have deigned to Bestow. The summer will not Be over Before I enjoy the delight to find myself under an American flag, on my way to the Beloved land of which it has been my Happy lot to Become an early soldier and an adopted son.

Be pleased Sir to accept my affectionate and grateful Respects.

LAFAYETTE.

LAFAYETTE TO MONROE.*

NEW YORK, August 18th 1824.

My dear Sir.

Here I am again, recast, on the Blessed Shore of America, where on the moment of my landing, I find myself Honored with new testimonies of your kindness. Some mistake in the information respecting the departure of the post Had prevented

*From State Dept. MSS., *Monroe papers.*

my writing yesterday, and the same morning your letter was delivered By Mr. Sam Goûveneur* and lieutenant Monroe. I Hope I will see them to day more at leisure as we met in very numerous Society, But will not delay this letter of mine with the enclosed from M.ʳ Brown.†

I came over with my Son who Requests His High and affectionate Regards be presented to you, and M. le Vasseur, a former officer in the French Army now my Secretary. We Had a short passage, and pleasant one as a fine ship, the *Cadmus*, excellent Captain, *Allyn*, and every accomodation and attention could make it. The only inconvenience that could not be obviated is sea sickness, of which we Had our full share.

The reception of me in this city I dare not dwell upon, as it looks like vanity, while I would like to express the feelings of gratitude, and all the delightful emotions that overwhelm my Heart. You will particularly sympathize in my sentiments at the meeting with our surviving Brother soldiers.

My dear friend, I am very anxious to embrace

---

*Mr. Monroe's second daughter, Maria, married Samuel L. Gouverneur, of New York. The latter was appointed Postmaster of that city by President John Quincy Adams. Later he served as an official in the Department of State from 1845 to 1849.

†James Brown, of Louisiana, United States minister to France from 1823 to 1829.

you: I wish it had been in my power to consult you before I had made my arrangements: I hope you will approve them.

The city of Boston had transmitted By the minister, Mr. Brown, an official kind invitation to make my first landing in that part of the union: I sent a respectful answer, intimating that whenever I should land, I would hasten to present, in person, my acknowledgments, and as Wednesday next is the time of what is called in the University of Cambridge, the *Commencement*, I will be arrived in Boston, By way of New Haven, New London and Providence, Before that day, then cross over to Albany and come down North River so as to be returned to New York in the first days of September. I have been informed through the governor of Virginia, there was to be a grand meeting of the Richmond, Norfolk and other volunteers at York town on the 19th October, where I am invited. My best plan I think would Be to leave New York about the middle of September, go to Philadelphia, Baltimore, Washington, where from, if I did not find you, it was my intention to Hasten to your country seat which in all cases I fondly Hope to visit as well as Montpellier and Monticello. Let me know, my dear Sir, whether this plan has your approbation.

Here are the two letters I have in charge for you: in my conversations with Mr. Brown, particularly the last, he expressed the great pleasure He found in Having with Him, as Secretary of Legation, Mr. Sheldon* whose utility to the embassy and to the minister He experienced every day. He requested me to mention it confidentially to you, but not knowing what arrangements might chance to take place in the interval between my arrival and our meeting, and Having myself an affectionate regard for Mr. Sheldon, I would not expose myself to the possible regret of Having delay'd for some weeks the confidential message entrusted to me.

Happy I am, my dear Sir, to be arrived under your presidency, Happy I will be to tell you, viva voce, How Respectfully, affectionately, and gratefully I am,

Your old Brother soldier and friend

LAFAYETTE.

My best respects to the ladies of the family.

LAFAYETTE TO MONROE.†

[WRITTEN EVIDENTLY Dec. 1824.]

My dear Friend:

I am delighted with your message and so will be every liberal mind in Europe and South America. As soon as I learned that a Committee Had been

---

* Daniel Sheldon, of Connecticut.

† From State Dept. MSS., *Monroe papers.*

appointed to regulate my reception in Congress I went to visit the members separately to show that I had Hitherto considered it as my only means to pay them my Respects and Acknowledgments: I Have also postponed every thought of excursion out of the city until I Hear from them ; it is thought by some they will do me the Honor to advise me on Monday: at all events I Have told my friends from Annapolis that I would not leave town before the Sixteenth, this even being submitted to the arrangements of Congress. I shall have the pleasure to dine with you, and arrive about four. My motive to wait for your usual dining Hour was the fear to take you from the business of the message. Most truly and affectionately

Your grateful friend

LAFAYETTE.

My two Companions will also avail themselves of your kindness to Have the Honor to dine with you.

Wednesday, morn.

LAFAYETTE TO MORGAN NEVILLE, ESQ.*

WASHINGTON Jany 16<u>th</u> 1825.

My dear Sir:

Since I Have Been denied the Happiness once

---

* The son of Genl. Presley Neville and grandson of Genl. Danl. Morgan.

more to embrace your father, my dear friend, aid, and Brother Soldier, I cannot now enjoy a Greater Satisfaction than to view His Lady, His Son, and all what Remains of His family. I Have Been inquiring after you from the moment of My Landing on the American Shore: the Relations of Nevill and Morgan cannot But Be Loved By me, and I am sure those feelings are Cordially Reciprocated.

The Letter you allude to Has not Been Received. The testimonies of affection I find in the name of your departed Brother and your own son are dear to my Heart. I anticipate the Gratification to see you all Before long.

It Has Been my intention to enjoy with the feelings of an American patriot those wonders of the West which I Have not Hitherto Been able to visit. Pittsburg and Cincinnati are two points I am particularly anxious to see; this double and very High gratification I shall obtain some time in the next Spring. I am Sorry to find my Journey must Be Rapid as I cannot Leave Here Before the Celebration of the 22^d February, and I am engaged to Be at Boston in time for the corner stone of the Bunker Hill Monument on the 17th June.

I will proceed to the Carolinas, Georgia, and across Alabama and Mississipi to New Orleans, thence to go up the two Great Rivers, so that I shall Have the pleasure to meet you at Cincinnati some time next Spring: I Have much felt, since your fine State of Ohio Has Been settled, for the prodigious Creations and Rapid improvements of that precious part of the Union: the Long wished for satisfaction will be greater on that account.

Receive, my dear Sir, the affectionate, and I am entitled to say the paternal Regard of your father's and your friend

LAFAYETTE.

GENERAL LAFAYETTE TO RICHARD FORREST.*

ALBANY, June 13th, 1825.

Dear Sir:

I Have Received on my arrival at this place Your kind favour and the letters that accompanied it. Mr. Clay Had informed me that such letters as Had a chance to meet me at Louisville were sent there; that the posterior packets were detained at Washington; He therefore invited me to ask their Being sent from the State office to any place where they could meet us. You know, my dear Sir, that those packets of letters, whatever Be their volume, Have Been Hitherto forwarded By the mail stage, nor do I understand in what other way I could get them. The letters I Have Received from family and friends allude to an anterior correspondence

---

* Richard Forrest was at that time an official in the Department of State.

the want of which Render part of them unintelli-
gible and unanswerable. I must therefore claim
your kindness to Have those packets sent to me as
soon and as safely as possible from Washington
and also from louisville, as you know in Whose
Hands they Have been deposited.

I am this morning setting out for Boston where
any thing you please to send will find me untill the
20th of this month. I shall Hence visit the States
of Maine, New Hampshire and Vermont so as to
Be Returned to Albany on the 29th On the 30th
evening I expect to go down the North River to
New York, paying some visits in my way But so
as to Reach the city two days Before the 4th July.
I Beg your pardon for the trouble I give you. But
you will [sic] Better than myself at which of those
places the letters from Washington and afterwards
those from Louisville can Best come to my Hands,
and I am sure you will kindly sympathize in my
eagerness to obtain them.

I need not observe that letters directed to my
son or to M. le Vasseur ought to be forwarded By
the mail. I will claim your kindness to Have them
convey'd to New York and directed to Mr Witt-
lock Junr at that place.

While I ought to apologise I will only thank you
for the trouble which you Have encouraged me to
give you, and of which, I confess, I stood in great
need Having no other way to Recover the series of

my correspondence from the other side of the
Atlantic.

With the Highest Regard I Have the Honor to
be

Yours

LAFAYETTE.

P. S. Upon consideration of the difficulties attending other Conveyances than the stage, I beg
you, my dear Sir, to keep at Washington the
trunks and other objects too Bulky to go By that
commodity. I expect to be at the seat of govmt.
about the middle of July.

LAFAYETTE'S ACKNOWLEDGMENT OF INDEBTED-
NESS TO MORGAN NEVILLE, ESQ.*

I Hereby acknowledge myself debtor to Morgan
Neville Esq. for the sum of four thousand dollars

---

*During his visit to America, Congress granted a tract of land
to General Lafayette. The act follows:

"*Be it enacted, &c.*, That the sum of Two Hundred Thousand
dollars be, and the same is hereby, granted to Major General
Lafayette, in compensation for his important services and ex-
penditures during the American Revolution, and that, for this
purpose, a stock to that amount be issued in his favor dated the
4th of July, 1824, bearing an annual interest of six per cent.
payable quarter yearly, and redeemable on the 31st December,
1834.

"Sec. 2. *And be it further enacted*, That one complete and
entire Township of Land be, and the same is hereby granted to
the said Major General Lafayette, and that the President of the

which I shall pay to Him in the course of three years from this day, the same sum Being in the mean while Mortgaged first on my *Florida township* the patent of which has been signed by the president of the U. S., two days ago, and a Second Mortgage on the *Capital* of $120,000 in the loan of the U. S., which capital is now under the management of the president of the U. S. Bank Who Has my power of attorney to send the Quarterly Rent to Europe. Done at Washington City under my Hand and Seal, August 7.th 1825.

LAFAYETTE.

POWER OF ATTORNEY FROM LAFAYETTE TO GEORGE GRAHAM, ESQ.*

Know all men by these presents, that

I, Lafayette, have made, constituted, and appointed, and by these presents do make, constitute, and appoint, George Graham, Esquire, of the

---

United States be authorized to cause the said Township to be located on any of the Public Lands which remain unsold, and that patents be issued to General Lafayette for the same," Passed December 23, 1824. *Congressional Debates, Vol. 1.*

*George Graham, of Va., was appointed Secretary of War. Apl. 7, 1817. He was afterwards President of the branch United States Bank in Washington, and in 1825 was appointed Commissioner of Public Lands, which position he held up to his death in 1830.

City of Washington in the District of Columbia, my true and lawful attorney, for me, and in my name, to lay out or cause to be laid out, all section number Thirty-one, in Township number One, North of Range number One, East of the Meridian Line, in the Land District of West Florida, or such part thereof as he may deem proper, into such Streets, Alleys, Town-lots or Out lots, and sell and dispose of the same, on such terms and conditions, as he may deem expedient, and to make all such deeds and conveyances as may legally be necessary and proper to convey the same, and generally to do and perform all such legal acts as may be necessary and proper to carry the full intention of this power of Attorney into effect, and one or more substitutes to appoint under him, and at pleasure revoke their powers. Hereby ratifying and confirming whatever my said attorney or his substitutes may legally do in the premises.

Given under my hand at the City of Washington, this second day of September, 1825.

Signed, sealed &
  delivered in
  presence of   LAFAYETTE.
    R. C. Weightman.

District of Columbia, City of Washington, D. C.

Be it remembered that on this 5th day of September 1825 General Lafayette personally appeared before the undersigned Mayor of the City of Wash-

ington, and acknowledged the within and forego-
ing Power of Attorney or Instrument of Writing,
to be his act and deed delivered for the purposes
therein mentioned.

In Testimony whereof I have hereunto subscribed my name, and caused the Seal
Washington ·
of the Corporation of the City of Washington aforesaid, to be affixed the date
City Seal
1802 · above written.

      R. C. WEIGHTMAN, Mayor.
Attest: WM. HEWITT, reg.

LAFAYETTE TO GEORGE GRAHAM.

[WASHINGTON, 1825.]

My dear Sir:

I think you may, in your kindness to me, call
this morning, and beg leave to inform you that I
must to day send to the post office my French letters, not a line of which has yet been begun. Could
I find you at your office to-morrow or the day following about two o'clock?

The more I reflect on your advice regarding
Florida and alternate lots the better it appears to
me. Will you please to talk of it with my excellent friend the president? Judge Duval who
knows much about Florida would also be a very
good adviser. Situated as I am, a set bargain for

that part of the lots would be more convenient than retailing them, provided it came up to or near to the value.

Your obedient and grateful friend,

LAFAYETTE,

Friday morn.

MONROE TO GEORGE GRAHAM.

OAK HILL, March 17, 1828.

Dear Sir :

Some late letters from Mr. Gamble, in Florida, give such favorable accounts of Gen! La Fayette's land, and of the probable rise of good land there, that the value, if these acc^{ts} are correct, cannot well be. estimated too high. This communication was made to me by Col. Mercer, of the H. of Reps., and lest it may not have reached you, I hasten to apprize you of it. He speaks of half a million of dolls., or more. Be so kind as to inform me whether any portion of it is sold. The General has written to me in a letter of Jany. 12th, respecting it, and in my answer I wish to give him the last information on the subject.

You have I presume received the copy of the memoir, which has been lately printed at the instance and under the direction of my friends in Albemarle. They allow me a large number of copies, which I shall distribute in a manner to make the subject thoroughly understood.   I think of having a copy delivered to each member of Congress before the adjournment, that the subject may be well understood by the next session, when it is hoped they will act on it.

Mrs. Monroe's health is improving, but so severe was the attack and so much reduced has she been by it, that her recovery is slow.   We have kept Hortensia as ignorant of it as we could.   The carriage goes for her to-morrow; we hope that you and your family are well.

Your friend,
JAMES MONROE.

LAFAYETTE TO MORGAN NEVILLE.

LAGRANGE, October 10th 1828.

My dear Sir:

I do not well know where this letter will Reach you Being intended to introduce Mr. Bowman who will visit Cincinnati after He has Remained some time in Orleans.   That gntleman is a painter, Born in the Western part of the Union, Having since inhabited Washington and the Atlantic Cities, who came to france and Has Remained Eight months in italy for improvement.   We Had the pleasure to see Him lately at LaGrange where He Has made three family portraits.   His character is much esteemed By His Country men in Europe and such other persons as he has been conversant with. I avail myself with much pleasure of this opportunity to offer you once more the affectionate Regards of

Your most sincere friend
LAFAYETTE.

LAFAYETTE TO MORGAN NEVILLE.

LAGRANGE, Novemb., 20, 1828.

My dear Sir:

It is to me a great gratification to hear of my Cincinnati friends. Still more so to Hear from them. I Hope this Letter will find you all in good Health; every account from the Westward delights me with a picture of the increasing extent and prosperity of your good, Beautiful City. I had lately written to Genl. Harrison at Columbia when I find He was likely, on the return of Mr. Poinsett, to go to Mexico. Cincinnati papers, when they come to me, are Highly welcome.

You are already informed, my dear sir, that my English friend, Mrs. Trolloppe with her family are your neighbors at Cincinnati. Had I known that was their destination I would, Before they left London Have given them Letters of introduction to you and Mrs. Neville. Her Husband, a respectable lawyer in the British Metropolis, is gone to join them Before I could avail myself of the opportunity; it is probable you have already Been long acquainted with them, nor do I know whether they are still on the Banks of the Ohio, in which case I Beg you to remember me to Her, and also to Her Husband and children. I have lately written to Her. Remember me also very affectionately to my friends in your kind family and in the City.

I have found out the Relatives of the traveller whom I could not But introduce on the spot when Requested By Him and knowing the acquaintance of which probably He availed Himself amidst the crowd of American friends By whom I Had the Happiness to Be surrounded. We shall meet them in town this winter and see what can Be done.

The Session of the Chamber des deputés will not open Before the end of January. I live in the country, as usual, in good health, the greater part of the family being with me. George and his wife are gone to Gueyenne South of france, to see their eldest daughter who is on the point of making me a great-grandfather. Mr Sparks is Here, Collecting information for his great work, which has given me an opportunity in the collection of my correspondence, to mention the dear name of my excellent friend Presley Neville. Ever truly and affectionately

Yours.

LAFAYETTE.

Morgan Neville, Esq.

MONROE TO GEORGE GRAHAM.

OAK HILL, Feby. 11, 1829.

Dear Sir:

I have received yours of the 6th with the document which you presented to the committee, who have my claims under consideration. It is correct in point of fact, for there was nothing that I could do at the awful moment when the President called me to the dept. of war, after the fall of the city that I did not do. I may say the same of my exertions at other difficult epochs of our country. In presenting that document in the manner you have done, you have I know the strong interest you take in my welfare.

I enclose you a letter which I have just received, under cover of one to me from General La Fayette. From his letter to me I infer the contents, which correspond with the relation which has existed between us since 1777. We were together and near each other in the battle of Brandywine when he rec^d his wound, and were afterwards together in that of Germantown and that of Monmouth, and we have preserved that friendly relation, as you well know, in every subsequent stage since. We found his wife in prison when we went to France, and aided in obtaining her release. I furnished her with funds and sent her to him to the prison of Olmutz, in Austria, where she remained with him several years until his discharge. On my second mission in 1803, I found him in Paris,. where our friendly intercourse was revived, and has always been preserved since. The good understanding and service rendered to his wife by mine is remembered by him. We have witnessed their distress and deeply sympathized for them. His present offer* is a repetition of one which he made me when with us. I told him that it was a generous one, in his situation, for I know with the [?] that would be made on him by visitors and his remaining creditors, that he would never be free from debt and trouble, and that sooner than receive it, I would perish. I begged him never to repeat it. I am gratified to find that he retains that friendly feeling for me, which however I never doubted, but my reply to him will be the same. I will answer him: you will consider this as the purport, unchangeable, of my answer, and take no step or make any arrangement in respect to his property in reference to me.

Very sincerely your friend,
JAMES MONROE.

---

* The offer was a pecuniary one. After his term as President Monroe's finances were much embarrassed. See his letter of May 22d.

MONROE TO GEORGE GRAHAM.

OAK HILL, May 4, 1829.

Dear Sir:

I have not heard from you of late, but hope that you and your family have enjoyed good health. I conclude that you have answered Genl. Lafayette's letter, offering aid to me by a pledge of his land in Florida, and assured him of my sensibility to the generous spirit which actuated him, but that I could never take from him or his family any portion of their property, having seen so much of their sufferings when I was in France, and having so strong a sense of his claims on our country and the friends of liberty everywhere.

I trust that you are under no apprehension respecting your situation. It appears to me impossible that you should have cause for it. Should you have any, and think that a desire [*sic*] to those in office, by you, to pronounce testimony of my confidence in your perfect integrity, capacity and diligence in the discharge of its duties would have a good effect, I wish you to intimate it to them. If either the President or a head of a Dept. will write me, I will give that answer, or, if on your intimations they should express a desire that you would produce such a document yourself and you will communicate the fact to me, I will send it instantly to you. You know that I can move, even in favor of those to whom I am most attached, in a particular way only, and I well know that out of that line my interference would not have a good effect.

Sincerely your friend,
JAMES MONROE.

MONROE TO LAFAYETTE.*

OAK HILL, May 22nd 1829.

My dear Friend:

It is some time since I wrote to you, in answer to your affectionate letters, although I have long intended to do it, and to acknowledge, that, particularly, in which you inclosed me one to Mr. Graham, but the feeling, which it excited, has in truth been the cause of the delay. So many interesting circumstances have occurred between us, to which we have been parties, and others of which we have been spectators, in both countries, since the battle of Brandywine, that I never can review them without peculiar interest and sensibility. The letter referred to, brought them to my recollection with great force. But, my dear friend, I can never take anything from you, nor from your family. I have known and seen too much of your and their sufferings, to commit such an outrage to my feelings. Your claims are too strong on me personally, on my country, and the friends of liberty everywhere, for me to do it. I sent your let-

---

* From State Dept. *MSS.*, *Monroe papers.*

ter to Mr. Graham, with instruction not to think of the measure, or rather to take no step in execution of it, and with which he has complied. If I was ever to visit France, your house would be my home, but we are both too far advanced in years to think of such a voyage. We must content ourselves with writing to each other, which I shall do hereafter, more frequently.

With my ill state of health, and the accident from which it proceeded in the first instance, you have been acquainted. I have suffered much thro' the winter, but am now so far recovered, as to be able to take my usual exercise on horseback, and which I do daily, when the weather will permit. The legislature of this state have called a convention, to be held in October next, to amend the Constitution. It was the first framed in the Union, and has managed affairs successfully; but it is generally admitted to have defects, which require amendment. Mr. Madison has been invited by his district to become a member, and to which he has consented, and will be elected. A like invitation has been given to me; in this I hesitated on account of ill health, but have at length expressed a willingness to serve if they desire it. I am personally little known in the district, and can therefore form no estimate of the result. My pursuits at home are interesting. My mind is not inactive, and in the employment given to it, a review of past

occurrences, in which I have acted, and of which I
have been a witness, occupies a large portion of
my time. I do not know that anything will appear to the public, during my life; but whenever it
does, should it be deemed worthy notice, a just regard will be shown to your services and claims, on
our countries, as well as to the friendly relations
which have existed between us & our families.

Mrs. Monroe and my whole family, take a deep
interest in the welfare and happiness of yours, as
well as in your own. All the details which you
give us respecting them are gratifying. Your own
health, we are happy to hear, is quite restored and
good. We hope that that of your son and daughters likewise is, and of their offspring. I sent to
Mr. Gouverneur, the papers you forwarded to me,
from the physicians in Paris, expressive of their
opinion respecting the infirmity of his son, & of
your desire to receive and render him any service
in your power, & for which he is most grateful.
The boy is at a school near the city of New York,
in which those thus afflicted are educated, and
his improvement is a cause of surprise, as well as
of consolation, to all the family. Should he ever
visit France, he will avail himself most willingly
of your good offices.

I will write you again soon. I have received
Mr. Marbois' book* relative to Louisiana. He

* *Histoire de La Louisiana et de la Cession de cette Colonie*

speaks of me with kindness & does justice to me, in many interesting circumstances, and as I believe to the full extent of his knowledge. There are some facts however, with which I am satisfied he was unacquainted. He states, for example, that he had commenc'd with Mr. Livingston, before my arrival in Paris in April 1803, and that he had done it in complyance with the instruction of Bonaparte, the first Consul. You will observe that the interview stated by Mr. Marbois, between the first consul and his two Ministers, took place on the tenth of April, on which day it was known to Mr. Livingsion & of course to the Govt., that I had arrived at Havre, & was on the route to Paris. The conference referred to is stated in page 285.* Mr. Livingston's letter in reply to mine, announcing my arrival, bears date likewise on the 10th, of which you will see a translation in page 468. If it was known to Mr. Livingston on the 10th that I had arrived, it must have been known to the first consul. It was known to all at Havre, as a salute was fired from the Battery and a guard of 50 men sent to the hotel where I stopped, whom I dismissed. That the first consul should have delayed his

___

par la France aux États-Unis de l'Amérique Septentrionale ; précédée d'un discours sur la constitution de le gouvernment des États-Unis. Par M. Barbé-Marbois. Paris, 1829.

* The references given by Mr. Monroe are correct according to the Paris Edition of 1829.

conference till that day is a proof of this fact; for otherwise, why did it not happen a day or a week before or after? He stated in the conference that coming 2,000 leagues, I must have now extensive powers, which shows that he waited for my arrival —page 267. He knew that nothing could be done till that event occurred. That he gave the instruction, as stated by Mr. Marbois, to proceed forthwith; I have no doubt, but that he gave it with a knowledge of the above facts, and with intention only to put the affair in train, I am equally confident.

In this circumstance, I think that Mr. Marbois is mistaken, as already observed, that he had commenced with Mr. Livingston, before my arrival. The day after my arrival, I dined with Mr. Livingston, having Col. Mercer and Mr. Skipwith with me, which was on the 12th or 13th of April, and while at dinner, Mr. Marbois arrived, & being informed that the family were at dinner, he walked in the garden until we arose from dinner. Mr. Livingston then joined him, and a conversation took place between them, in which it was agreed, that they should have an interview that night, at Mr. Marbois' house, which took effect. According to my recollection Mr. Marbois retired without seeing me, & as I presume without knowing that I had arrived. I well recollect, that after his departure, Mr. Livingston disclosed the fact of his appointment, with many other circumstances, of which he had just been informed by Mr. Marbois, and of which he knew nothing before, his whole conversation having been of a different cast, predicting the impossibility of a satisfactory termination of the mission; and in the presence of Col. Mercer and Mr. Skipwith, I proposed to accompany Mr. Livingston, in the interview with Mr. Marbois, having known him since the year 1783, at Annapolis, and been much with him, in my first mission to France, and having personal regard for, & confidence in him; but to this he objected. Mr. Livingston had not then read his instructions, which was an additional motive for wishing to accompany him, in the interview, to guard against his compromitment of himself. Many other circumstances of a like kind, in support of what is above noticed, occurred, and of which I have proof, which has never been stated, or published, to promote any object, on my part, either of advancement or fame, altho' they have been called for, by misrepresentation here. It is admitted that a war with England menaced, but it appears by Mr. Marbois' statement that that was considered as certain as early as Jany., and was deemed inevitable, soon afterward, if not before. Mr. Marbois states on page 275, that before the message of the King of England of the 8th of March, 1803, the first consul had considered the war inevitable. Mr. Talleyrand's letter to Mr. Livingston, of the 24th of

March, declaring that he should wait my arrival, is a farther proof that the first consul knew the fact, and gave his instructions to Mr. Marbois in consequence thereof. The order to Bernadotte which you communicated to me, to leave Paris, the day I entered it, shews that he was acquainted with it, & intended to prevent an interview between him and me.

If you see no impropriety in it, I have no objection to your shewing to Mr. Marbois, what I have stated above. I wish nothing but the truth, in which I am satisfied he concurs. A communication took place between him & me on this subject, before my retirement, in which I stated to him at his request, some facts, particularly the letter of Mr. Talleyrand to Mr. Livingston of 24th of March, & Mr. Livingston's letter to me of the 10th of April, which he has published.

I have entered further into this subject, than I intended, but I have done it, from a knowledge of the interest which you take in what relates to my welfare and character. Retired now from public life, with no desire ever to enter it again, I can have no object, in what relates to the past, than a strict regard to justice. Let me hear from you as soon as convenient, and give us all the details mentioned, respecting your family as well as yourself. Our affectionate regards to you and them.

Very sincerely your friend

JAMES MONROE.

LAFAYETTE TO MONROE.*

PARIS, June 17, 1829.

My dear Friend:

A long, very long while Has elapsed since I Had
the pleasure to Hear from you. I Hope However
you Have received my letters, namely those Relative to your poor grand son and to your own affairs
which give me great uneasiness. I have Had, in
the case of the Boy, every inquiry, every consulta-
tion in my power, the Result of which Has Been
that the Bruxelles practice is but an emanation ot
the new Parisian methods, not so wonderful as Has
Been Reported, But greatly improved from the
ancient mode of treatment. Two eminent physicians and Surgeons Have especially applied their
talents to that object, But it is necessary, they say,
to Have a personal view of the patient until a
guess can be formed—it appears also that in cases
unfortunately too common, where a cure cannot
be obtained, they Have devised means to make the
situation less uncomfortable. It Had made me Hope
to see some of the family at paris and La Grange,
But [no] information of the kind Has.yet reached
me.

I have been much pleased to Hear that the two
Virginia ex-presidents Have accepted a seat in the
State Convention With a sense of Virginian pride
I anticipate the result; this new constitution, after

---

* From State Dept. *MSS.*, *Monroe papers.*

a political experience of fifty years, in the several
parts of the Union, cannot but offer a model of
social organization, so far as it can Be the case
under the lamentable evil of negro slavery, en-
tailed, forced upon the colony By the mother country, a check upon agriculture, an object of continued
reproach and regret, yes of incommensurable difficulty to remove it. Oh, How proud and elated I
would feel, if something could be contrived in your
convention whereby Virginia, who was the first to
petition against the slave trade, and afterwards to
forbid it, who Has published the first declaration of
Rights, would take an exalted situation among the
promoters of measures tending first to meliorate,
then gradually to abolish the slave mode of labour.
You know how anxious our departed friends were
on this subject, altho' they were sensible of the ob-
stacles.   But could not something be done point-
ing that way and announcing the principles and
feelings which I Have submitted on that score in
the Southern States, with a determination to enter
the road to improvement, and finally attain, if possible, the desirable end?   In addition to my painful
anxiety with respect to your pecuniary embarrass-
ments, upon which I Have formerly and fully
written to you,* I Have had my fears relative to
the state of your Health until I have been assured

* The letter referred to is not among the Monroe papers.

it was fully Restored. There have been other causes of friendly uneasiness such as the Rumor that Has Been spread of a change in the post mastership of N. Y.,* and altho' I could not believe it I felt a letter from you at the time would have been particularly welcome.

Our friend Nich douglass is gone to revisit Great Britain. I shall as soon as the Chambre des deputes Rise go with George and His daughters on a visit to my dear grand daughter Natalie perier, so as to be returned to La Grange in the Beginning of September. The public papers in France, if you read some of them, particularly "the Courier and Constitutionel," may give you some account of interior affairs, and what relates to european politics is either translated, or if english, copied in the American papers. I However inclose what I had occasion to say at the French tribune, as it recalls an interesting epoch, and refers to the Bill of the *double vote* the greatest nuisance in the electoral legislation of this country.

Mr. Brown and His lady are preparing to leave us. Their departure depends, as to the time, upon Mrs. Brown's state of Health. They are much regretted. We Have Been very sorry to Hear Mr.

---

* Mr. Governeur, Mr. Monroe's son-in-law, who had been appointed by President J. Q. Adams, was then Postmaster at New York.

Beasly * consul at Havre is removed, it is the case also they say with old Mr. Murray † at Liverpool. The last account from America says Mr. Rives ‡ is appointed to France. Governor Barbour || Had neither asked nor declined a continuation in office. He is expected Here as a visitor at the end of this month. How is Mrs. Monroe? present my most tender respects to Her.

Altho' the other powers endeavor to obtain a peace between Russia and Turkey it is probable they will try the fate of war; the diplomacy of france Has been more sincere and liberal than that of the British government. We wish the ministry and King not to go out of the line of independance, Having nothing to do either with the Belligerents or the other powers. England Has been Backward in everything respecting the limits or welfare of Greece, and I fear this cabinet will adhere to contracted views; they contemplate to have Greece a tributary to the porte, confined to a small area saddled with a sort of Hereditary monarch.

Adieu, my dear excellent friend, present my most affectionate Respects to Mrs. Hay, § Mrs.

---

* Reuben G. Beasley, of Va., appointed Jany. 2, 1817.

† James Maury, of Va., appointed June 7, 1790.

‡ William C. Rives, of Va., appointed April 18, 1829.

|| James Barbour, of Va., then Minister to England.

§ Mr. Monroe's elder daughter, Eliza, married George Hay, afterwards Judge of the Eastern District of Virginia. Their

Governeur, their Husbands, and dear Hortensia, in which George joins with all the affection of His feelings for you and for them. You know How affectionately I am

Your old friend

LAFAYETTE.

LAFAYETTE TO MONROE. *

PARIS, 7ᵇʳ 8, 1830.

My dear Friend:

Your warm interest in the fate of French freedom will have made you a hearty partaker in the triumph of the popular cause;† it is exquisitely the victory of the people. The name of your old Brother soldier Has been the rallying signal; But no other merit Belongs to the chief. Hundred Battles were fought at once in every quarter of the city; the moment I heard at LaGrange of the ordinance I posted up to town; the action Began the same evening; the 28 & 29ᵗʰ were too Bloody days, in the morning of the 29ᵗʰ the three colored flag and my Headquarters were planted at the Hotel de Ville,

---

daughter, whom General Lafayette alludes to, was called Hortensia, after Queen Hortense, with whom Eliza Monroe had gone to Mme. Campan's School in Paris. See Gilman's *Monroe.*

* From State Dept. MSS., Monroe papers.

† The allusion is to the Revolution of August, 1830, which placed Louis Phillippe, the citizen king, upon the throne.

the next morning the royal family and troops were
at St. Cloud and I was enabled to write by a flag
they Had ceased to Reign. They stopped at Ram-
bouillet with the hopes of a Civil war, their army
was twelve thousand, I some twenty thousand par-
isians, George marched with them, but Before an action took place they renounced their warlike plan,
gave up the jewels of the crown and went on slowly
to Cherbourg under the protection of our three
commissioners, whence they embarked for england.
Not a word of insult, none of those acts that you
Have seen in the former scenes of the french revolution. All bravery, skill, disinterested generosity.
We are organizing the national guards, and in
three weeks time fifty thousand men were received
in the champ de Mars. You will, I think, approve
the resolution taken by us Republicans, in the
present exterior and interior circumstances, to adhere to the will of the well known majority of the
nation, and to have a popular throne surrounded
with popular institutions. No better King and son
can evèr exist. You remember Philipp the 1ˢᵗ was
the young Republican and milder soldier, Duke
de Chartres. So we stand now, not doing the best
that can be wished, but doing well, and progressing
on a good road of political improvement. You will
have perceived that in the sitting relative to the
recognition of South America and Mexican independence, justice Has been done to the priority of

the U. S. over all other powers; there is, of course some revolutionary excitement among our neighbors, france will not allow foreign intervention, thereby following the principle of your celebrated message.

Present my affectionate Respects to Mrs. Monroe, to your daughter and her Husband, to Dear Hortensia in whose fate and change of name I Have felt tenderly and paternally interested. I Have also considered it as a Happy event for Mrs. Eliza Custis' grand children and for herself. My family beg to be most respectfully remembered. George shares with me the cares of this important situation where the fate of European liberty is so highly concerned.

Your old affectionate friend
LAFAYETTE.

GENERAL NATHANIEL ROCHESTER.

AUTOBIOGRAPHY OF NATHANIEL ROCHESTER.*

I was born in Westmoreland County, Virginia, on the 21st of February, 1752.   *   *   *   *   *
In 1775 I was appointed a member of the Committee of Safety for Orange County,† whose business was to promote the revolutionary spirit among the people, to procure arms and ammunition, make

---

*The autobiography of Nathaniel Rochester may be supplemented by the following facts. "While living in that place [Hagerstown] he became in succession a member of the Maryland assembly, postmaster, and judge of the county court, and in 1808 he was chosen a presidential elector, and voted for James Madison. * * * * In 1800 he first visited the 'Genesee country,' where he had previously bought 640 acres, and in September of that year he made large purchases of land in Livingston county, N. Y., near Dansville, in connection with Major Charles Carroll, Col. William Fitzhugh and Col. Hilton. In 1802 he purchased, jointly with Carroll and Fitzhugh, the '100-acre or Allan Mill tract,' in Falls Town (now Rochester), and in May, 1810, he removed from Hagerstown and settled near Dansville, where he remained five years * * * * and in April, 1818, took up his residence in Rochester, which had been named for him." He filled a number of important local offices afterwards, and died in Rochester May 14, 1831 (see Appleton's Cyclopaedia of American Biography).

† North Carolina. Rochester had removed to that colony a few years before.

collections for the people of Boston, whose harbour was blocked up by the British fleet, and to prevent the sale and use of East India teas. In August of the same year, 1775, I attended as a member of the first Provincial Convention in North Carolina. This convention ordered the raising of four regi‑ments of Continental troops, organized the minute men and militia systems, and directed an election for another convention to meet in May, 1776, for the purpose of forming and adopting a constitution and form of government and measures of defence. At this first convention I was appointed a *Major of Militia*, *Paymaster* to the minute men and militia, and a Justice of the Peace.

In February, 1776, the commander of the British forces in New York sent General Alexander Mc‑Donald to Cumberland County, in North Carolina, the inhabitants of which county were mostly High‑land Scotch, who had fled from Scotland for their adherence to the Pretender to the Crown of England in 1745; and so secret were his proceedings that be‑fore it was known in other parts of the province he had raised 1,000 men and formed them into a regi‑ment and had them ready to march for Wilming‑ton, at the mouth of Cape Fear River (about 100 miles), where transports from New York were to meet them. As soon as information of these move‑ments reached Hillsborough, a distance of about 80 miles, the minute men and militia of Orange and Granville Counties collected and marched down to Cross Creek (now Fayetteville), the seat of justice of Cumberland County, where it was understood McDonald and his regiment of tories were embodied. I went with the minute men and militia in my official capacities as Major and Paymaster, and on our arrival at Cross Creek we heard that McDonald and his regiment had set out a few days before for Wilmington to embark for New York. I was then dispatched by Col. Thackston, our commanding officer, at 8 o'clock at night, with two companies of infantry and one company of cavalry, in pursuit of the enemy; but on our arrival about daybreak at Devo's Ferry, about 20 miles from Cross Creek, or headquarters, we met about 500 men with General McDonald on their retreat, they having been met and defeated at Moore's Creek Bridge by Col. Caswell,* commander of a

---

* " The provincial parties were, however, so close in the pursuit, and so alert in cutting the country and seizing the passes, that McDonald at length found himself under a necessity of engaging a Colonel Caswell, who, with about a thousand militia and minute men, had taken possession of a place called Moore's Creek Bridge, where they had thrown up an intrenchment. The royalists were, by all accounts, much superior in number, having been rated from 3000 to 1500, which last number, McDonald, after the action, acknowledged them to be. * * * But McLeod, the second in command, and a few more of their bravest officers and men, being killed at the first onset, they suddenly lost all spirit, fled with the utmost precipitation, and as the provincials say, deserted their General, who was taken

regiment of minute men. Col. Caswell was afterwards appointed the first Governor of the State. We took the 500 prisoners. Being, however, in a sparsely settled country, where provisions could not be obtained, I was obliged to discharge all but about 50, who were appointed officers by McDonald, after swearing those discharged that they would not again take arms against the United Colonies; notwithstanding which they did afterwards join Lord Cornwallis when he marched through North Carolina, in the year 1782.

I then returned to headquarters with my command and the fifty prisoners, where I found Col. Alex. Martin, of the Salisbury Minute Men, had arrived with about two thousand minute men and militia. He took the chief command.

Marshall, in his life of Washington, mentions that Martin took these prisoners. They were sent under a guard as prisoners of war to Frederick Town, in Maryland, where they remained until exchanged. In disarming the prisoners at Devo's ferry, the Scotch gave up their dirks with much reluctance, they having, as they said, been handed down from father to son for many generations.

---

prisoner, as were nearly all their leaders, and the rest totally broken and dispersed." Quoted in Revolutionary History of North Carolina from the *Annual Register* for 1776. Marshall's recount of this affair does not differ materially from the above. It is not stated by him that Col. Alex. Martin took the prisoners.

In May following, 1776, when I was 24 years of age, I attended the convention at Halifax, N. C., as a member, when a constitution or form of government was adopted. Six more regiments of Continental troops were ordered to be raised, and their officers appointed, among whom I was appointed *Commissary General of military stores and clothing*, with the *rank and pay of* a *Colonel* for *the North Carolina line*, which consisted of ten regiments.

This convention organized a government by appointing a governor and other State officers, and directed an election in November following for members of a State legislature.

On the adjournment of the convention I set out for Wilmington, N. C., where the four regiments first raised were stationed, in order to attend to the duties of my office, and took with me Abishia Thomas as a deputy, who was allowed the pay of a subaltern officer, and who has since been a clerk in one of the departments of the General Government. After riding to most of the seaport towns in Carolina and Virginia to procure military stores and clothing for the Army, I was taken sick at Wilmington, and unable to transact business for a considerable time. My physician and friends advised me to retire from the service, on account of my condition and the unhealthiness of that part of the country. I therefore resigned a week or two before the election for members of the legislature, but did not return to Hillsborough until some weeks after the election. On my return there, I found that I had been elected a Member of the Assembly, which I attended in the winter of 1777, with Nathaniel Macon, who had, a little before the election, returned home from Princeton College, and was elected to the same Assembly. He has since been a member of Congress for about thirty years without intermission. During this session I was appointed *Lieutenant Colonel of Militia*, and in the spring following, Clerk of the Court of Orange County, which office had been held many years by Gen'l F. Nash, who was killed at the battle of German Town. I held the clerk's office about two years, and until the fees of the office did not pay for the stationery used, owing to the depreciation of the paper currency.

This year, 1777, I was appointed a Commissioner to establish and superintend a manufactory of arms at Hillsborough, and went to Pennsylvania with several wagons for bar iron for the factory. When I resigned the clerk's office I was appointed one of a board of three Auditors of Public Accounts for the State, and a Colonel of Militia.

In 1778 I engaged in business with Col. Thos. Hart (Henry Clay's father-in-law,) and James Brown, our present minister to France. Col. Hart resided two miles west of Hillsborough, where he had a considerable estate in land, mills and other manufacturing establishments. His residence was about on the line between the Whig and Tory settlements; the Tories committed many depredations on his property, he being a very influential and active Whig. There were frequent instances of the Whigs and Tories not only committing depredations on each other in North and South Carolina, but murdering people along their borders. Gen. Gates, who in 1779 commanded the Southern army, advised Col. Hart to remove with his family to Berkley county, Virginia, where the family of the General resided, and as Col. Hart's property and his life was endangered by remaining where he was, he took the advice of the General and in the autumn of 1780 removed not to Berkley but to Hagers Town in Maryland, being in an adjoining county though a different State. Col. Hart prevailed upon me to accompany him, proposing and promising to go into mercantile business in Philadelphia. Soon after we arrived at Hagers Town he furnished the capital promised, and I proceeded to Philadelphia by way of Baltimore (then a small place), in February, 1781, and took lodging at the "Canastoga Wagon," a first rate tavern at that time.

CÆSAR RODNEY.

CÆSAR RODNEY TO CAPTAIN THOMAS RODNEY.*

PHILADA Sept 25th 1776.

Sir:

That the New England men failed to defend the Landing place,† Behaved in a most Dastardy Cowardly Scandalous manner is most Certain. But that courage is not always to be found the same, even in the same person is equally true, and veryfied in those very same men, for some of them the day following were in the other engagement and

---

* Cæsar Rodney, of Delaware, took his seat in Congress on Sept. 5, 1774, with Thomas McKean as his colleague, and was a Signer of the Declaration of Independence. While absent in Philadelphia he was appointed a Brigadier General by Delaware. The letter to his brother, Captain Thomas Rodney, was written from Congress, shortly before his retirement from that body, while the letter to General Smallwood was written just after Rodney's election to the Presidency of Delaware, which office he held for four years. In Niles' *Principles and Acts of the Revolution* (p. 245, edition of 1876) will be found further correspondence between Cæsar and Thomas Rodney.

† The allusion is to the struggle for the Hudson. The British landed in force on the August 22, and drove Col. Hand's regiment back. The fighting continued for several days, ending in the occupation of New York by the enemy.

behaved with great Bravery, as did the whole Body engaged; you have some account of the skirmish in the papers therefore shall refer you to them, and a Letter I wrote by Wilds & Richley—I saw Carsons, but not till this morning when he told me some person by the name of Jones from Mifflins Corps had set out from below since he did and having got here before him with subscription papers signed by some people below went to the several printing offices before he did and engaged the packets to carry down as a post in the Island of Parke. After I saw Bradford the [sic] and telling them what accounts I had from below and what Carson himself had said He said they would let Carson have the papers for the Gentlemen of Dover and elsewhere, except those who subscribed to the other. I suppose the subscribers will settle the matter between them, when they go down—I doubt whether you will get any powder & shott— The schooner is not arrived that I know of,—and you have made no mention of the sloop—but sent the schooner before you heard what my opinion was about selling her. I wrote you concerning them both by Richly—My Pen is confounded Bad. I am too blind to mend it,* and Captain Paploy

---

* Rodney suffered from his youth with a cancer of the left side of his face, and for many years before his death wore a green silk screen over it. It would appear that the disease had affected his vision.

who mends and makes them for me is gone out—
therefore must bid you farewell.

CÆSAR RODNEY.

P. S.   The convention is dissolved, made a plan
of Government it seems and ordered an Election at
a short day—Query, do their late opponents intend
calmly to submit, or try again to Rally—I am
sorry for Mr. Pillows Illness.

Thomas Rodney, esq.

CÆSAR RODNEY TO GENL. SMALLWOOD.

DOVER, April the 28th 1778.

Sir:

Suppressing the Insurrection of the Villian Clow
and his ragged Gang* has almost exhausted the
little ammunition I had, and not knowing where
it may be possible, Immediately, to procure a supply of that necessary article, has constrained me to
report my application to you—I am now reduced,
I believe, to about Three Rounds, and therefore
must beg you immediately to use your utmost endeavour to supply me with cartridges or Powder

---

*Rodney wrote under date of May 8, 1778, to McKean, then
in Congress: "We are constantly alarmed by the Enemy and
refugees, and seldom a day passes, but some man in this and
the neighboring counties is taken off by these villains: so that
many near the bay, dare neither act or speak lest they should
be taken away and their houses plundered."   Sanderson's
American Biography, Vol. VIII, p. 112 (Edition of 1827).

and Lead unmade up.   I rest assured that your attachment to the cause and Willingness to oblige me will induce you to Comply without loss of time.

              I am Sir Your most

                    obed.ᵗ Humb.ˡ Servt

                          CÆSAR RODNEY.

Genl. Smallwood.

D.ᴿ NATHANIEL SCUDDER.*

ACTION OF COMMITTEE OF MONMOUTH COUNTY.

In consequence of an Advertisement from the New Jersey Committee of Correspondence, a full and well authenticated Representation of the several Townships of Middle Town, Freehold, Upper Freehold, Dover and Stafford appeared at the Court House in Freehold on Thursday the 10ᵗʰ of May 1775, and without Dissent placed John Anderson Esq.ʳ in the Chair.

A number of gentlemen attended from the Township of Shrewsbury under the Character of Deputies of the Shrewsbury association, declaring

---

* In 1776 D.ʳ Nathaniel Scudder, of Monmouth Court House, N. J., was made Lieut. Col. of the Monmouth Co. Militia, under Colonel George Taylor, and succeeded to the command when Taylor renewed his allegiance to the king and went over to the enemy. In November, 1777, Scudder was elected delegate to the Continental Congress, and served till 1782. His county was frequently excited by excursions of British forage parties, and in an engagement on Oct. 16, 1781, with refugees near Shrewsbury, he was killed while leading a batallion. (See *Pennsylvania Magazine*, Vol. III, p. 189; also Moore's *Diary of the American Revolution*, Vol. II, p. 504, for manner of Scudder's death.)

themselves and their Constituents desirous of adopting the measures of the late Continental Congress and willing to acceed to any future Plan for the general safety and Well being of America, who were cordially received by the Committees of the other Towns as Exempts from the Township in which they resided.

They furthermore advised them to appear at the provincial Convention at Trenton, and there fairly represent a State of their Case, promising them their friendly Concurrence in whatever should there be adopted as a mode of Relief to them from the public Censure incurred by the Inhabitants of Shrewsbury—

The Committees of the above mentioned five Townships, being a great Majority of the County of Monmouth, conceived themselves vested with ample Power to constitute Deputies to represent said County at the approaching provincial Convention at Trenton, and accordingly elected the following Gentlemen, any three of whom shall be a sufficient number to attend for that Purpose, viz: John Taylor Esq., Capt John Covenoven, Mr. John Holmes, Mr Joseph Saltar, and Mr. Robert Montgomery, who are fully authorized by their Constituents to meet and consult with the Deputies of the other Counties in the Colony of New Jersey, and these with them to concert and adopt any such Measures, as shall by a Majority of that convention be deemed conducive to the general Security of American Freedom.

Signed by Order of said Committees

NATHANIEL SCUDDER Clerk.

Freehold May 18th 1775.

D^R. NATHANIEL SCUDDER TO ——————.

FREEHOLD, March 28th, 1777.

Sir:

Late last evening I rec'd yours of the 19th Instant respecting the Cargo of the Schooner Betsey which was stranded at long Branch in Shrewsbury in this County & in answer thereto have the Mortification to inform you that the Enemy while they had Possession of the County seized and appropriated the greatest Part of it, insomuch, that upon the Best Inquirey, I can never since hear of more than the Fustick & Staves which are considerable squandered, and of about 30 Casks of oil and ninety odd Barrels of the Pot or Pearl Ash which are gone to Philadelphia; when I had the Pleasure of seeing Mr Patten in Philadelphia, this whole County was under the Dominion of the Tories and was disarmed & made a scene of Devastation. Soon after the memorable Battle of Princeton Genl Putnam detached a Party of Militia under the Command of Col. Francis Gurney of Philadelphia, who marched

them into Monmouth, routed the Tories and seized
a considerable Quantity of stores in several Places.
I myself marched with the same Detachment and
continued with them untill the enemy were entirely dispersed & their stores at Middle Town
seized, when I was obliged to attend constantly at
Freehold both on account of furnishing Teams to
haul them off & to endeavour to revive and rally
the militia of the County; so that I was not at
Shrewsbury when Col. Gurney took possession of
the stores there—However upon leaving there were
a Quantity of Spermaceti Oil, Pot or Pearl ash
among them. I immediately applied to Col.
Gurney, and informed him, that I expected it
was a Part of the Cargo of the Schooner aforsd,
and put in a Claim in behalf of the owners,
at the same time protesting in their favour against
the sale of said Articles, other than for their Benefit — I afterwards saw some of s^d oil & ash
on the way to Philadelphia and have no doubt of
its being a Part of s^d Cargo, but the Confusion of
the time has been such that I have never been
able fully to ascertain the matter. Mr. Patten said
that after the schooner stranded she fell into the
hands of our Militia, who, (as there was no Court
of Admiralty in this State, nor any Disposition of
s^d Cargo ordered until too late); kept the Cargo
well guarded until the sudden Irruption of the
enemy in to these parts, when they were obliged

to quit it & provide for themselves. Col. Georgie Taylor, in whose charge it was, and who has proved himself a Traitor to his Country & is gone over to the enemy, immediately seized the whole of s^d Cargo in the King's name and improved his time so well that the Articles before mentioned were all that can since be heard of. He and his Genl. have doubtless appropriated all the most valuable Part, & put the Proceeds in their Packet. Soon after the Removal of the s^d stores I was obliged to meet the Council of this State & have been closely ingaged ever since untill yesterday morning when I returned home. In order, however, that every thing might be done that could be, I spoke to the Commissioners and desired them to consult the Interest of the owners in the disposition of the oil & ash which they promised to do—The issue I know not—I at the same time desired Levi Cook to take care of the Fustick and Staves that he might receive the Cost he had been at in unloading & Removing the Cargo, & preserve the Remainder for the owners, which he undertook. But unfortunately some few weeks after he with a large Guard were surprised near Sandy Hook and a great Number of them taken Prisoners, who yet remain in captivity, so that I know not what he has done in the affair. I expect to go to Shrewsbury to morrow and shall enquire about the Fustick & staves. This is the best account I am at present able to give you & must leave yon to act as you think proper.

         I am Sir Your Very obbt servt,

                  NATH. SCUDDER.

excuse the great haste & hurry.

P. S. By applying to Col: Gurney in Philadelphia you may probably be informed wether the oil & ash are sold or not.   N. S.

GENERAL CHARLES LEE.

GENERAL CHARLES LEE TO JAMES MONROE.*

BERKLEY COUNTY, June ye 25th 1780.

My dear Monroe:

I received two days ago your letter dated from Richmond upbraiding me for not writing—I do assure you that I have written twice immediately addressed to you, and third time addressed to you Conjointly with Mercer—but whether you have received em I can not pretend to say, as amongst the many admirable qualities possessed by the Inhabitants of this Continent, the noble ambition of opening every letter, in order to obtain knowledge, is one of the most predominant—it is not always that I am master of pen ink and paper, and seldom that I have an opportunity of aprising you how much and sincerely I am yours, or you may depend upon it that you should receive these assurances very frequently, as without compliment there are few young men for whom I have a higher esteem and affection—I am certainly concerned that Fortune has been so unkind as not to admit

---

* Compare the letter from Lee to Monroe printed on page 278 *et seq.*, Vol III (Lee Papers) New York Historical Society's publications.

of your cultivating the talents which Nature has bestowed on you to greater advantage than your present situation seems to Promise, for in my opinion (but perhaps I am a prejudiced man) the study of topographical Law (unless daily corrected by other more liberal studies) is a horrid narrower of the mind; and you, as you justly complain, have not the proper books for this necessary correction. If I remain on the Continent nothing will give me greater pleasure, or more flatter my ambition, than to communicate my ideas and assist you with all the means in my power in your pursuit of polite letters,—and if any circumstances arise to make me alter my present plan, I hope it may be so contrived that we may be much together. Your present Assembly, I have many reasons to believe, is composed of most wretched materials, but wretched as it is, I have as many reasons to believe, that it is one of the least abominable on the Continent—in fact, the power in every State is fallen into the very worst hands. We have now neither monarchy, Aristocracy, nor Democracy; if it is any thing, it is rather a Mac-ocracy, by which I mean that a Banditti of low Scotch-Irish who are either themselves imported servants or the immediate descendants of Imported Servants are the Lords Paramount, and in such wild beastly hands as these respublica diutius stare non potest. God knows what is to become of us; I possibly see with a jaundiced eye, but I am myself fully persuaded that after some months or at highest a couple of years' anarchy and confusion, an absolute Tyranny will be the conclusion of the Piece; but whether the Tyrant will be foreign or domestic is out of the reach of foresight. What do you think of the policy of virtue of Congress, in inviting (or if not invited), in admitting a large Body of French Troops into our bosom—How are We to get rid of 'em? Is there an instance in history of a strong nation sending an Army for the protection of an impotent one, when the Protectors have not ultimately stripped or attempted to strip the Protected of their liberties? You have, I am sure, read the history of Britain, and must be acquainted with the conduct of our Saxon Ancestors—You have likewise probably read the history of Charles the Fifth and Philip the Second, and of course, must know that the Armies of Germans Italians and Spaniards introduced under the pretext of protecting the Low Countries against the French were Employed to Capture these very Low Countries, and that afterwards vice versa the French, called on to protect Em from the tyranny of the Spaniards and Italians, attempted to accomplish the very same purposes. They were called in to defeat—in short the measure is so very big with myschief, so repugnant to the first axioms of policy, that I cannot. . must have been bribed out of the little sense they set out with—but I am warmed by the subject into a tedious political essay—it has been revealed * to Mrs. Gates in a dream that S. Carolina is of not the least importance, which revelation She has communicated to the General to his unspeakable comfort; the General has communicated it to a McAllaster and the other Commissaries, who have comforted the whole County with the glad tidings —and it is resolved by a Committee of whigs, that whoever insinuates that S. Carolina and the Army taken in it, are of the least consequence, is *ipso facto* a damn'd Tory.   Upon my word I pity Gates. He is an honest man and has many good qualities, and that Dæmoness his wife occasions him to make a very rediculous figure—Adieu, God bless you.

C. LEE.

P. S.† I suppose an Army of Russians will likewise be introduced as well as an Army of French, and then the Country will be a blessed theatre of war and desolation; one side or the other must be victorious, or it must be a drawn battle; if the former happen, the victor will dictate what measures He pleases, and if the latter happen, a treaty of partition will take place.   Upon the whole it is a damnable measure.

---

* This language and what follows is not found in the letter printed in the N. Y. Historical Society's collection.

† The strictures on the French army appear in the body of the N. Y. Historical Society's letter.

GENERAL GEORGE WEEDON.

FREDERICKSBURG, May 3^d 1781.

Sir:

I am favored with yours 27th ult.? respecting the powder belonging to Government. The cause of my altering the rout of the waggons carrying supplies to Genl. Greens Army, was in consequence of the Enemies being in James River; they were positively Directed via Richmond, where the

---

* George Weedon was Lieut. Col. of the 3^d Virginia Regiment in 1776, and afterwards held the same rank in the 1st Virginia Regt. Feby. 23, 1777, he was commissioned a Brigadier General, and participated in the battles of Brandywine and Germantown. Shortly after the latter battle he retired from the Army, owing to a question of disputed rank, and did not serve again, until the Yorktown Campaign, when he was in command of of a brigade and had charge of the Virginia Militia at Gloucester. Appleton's *Cyclopædia of American Biography.*

† William R. Davie entered the Army in 1776 as a volunteer, was elected lieutenant of a troop of horse in 1779 and attached to Pulaski's legion. He rose to the rank of Major and was wounded at Stono, near Charleston. In 1780 he raised a troop of horse, was at the battles of Hanging Rock, Ramsour's Mills, and Charlotte. Genl. Greene appointed him commissary of the Southern Army, and he was at the engagements at Guilford, Hobkirk's Hill, and Ninety-Six. Lossing's *Pictorial Field Book of the Revolution*, Vol. II, pp 418, 419.

powder was ordered to be left. My knowledge of
the Scarcity of that article induced me to stop it
here till further Directions, for fear of a misfortune,
that would have proved fatal. It was immediately
on rect of yours, sent off to Carters Ferry where I
hope it is Deposited in safety. Just before I left
Williamsburg had the pleasure of communicating
to his Excellency the Governor an offer made me by
Mr. Best of the Loan of some powder & lead belonging to him, which I conceived in the time of
distress worthy the attention of Government. I
known not whether they accepted his offer. If they
did not, I dare say it may still be had if wanting.
We have abundant reasons to believe Sr Harry
Clinton is meditating a sudden descent somewhere
to the Southward. An Embarkation of 3000 men
is taking at N: York perhaps destin'd for Virg^a,
therefore be prepared if possible. You need not
expect the Second Division soon. Indeed the best
policy is to depend upon ourselves, as our allies
have no doubt great objects of their own to attend
too. Genl. Wayne has marched with 1200 of the
Penn^s line, Maryland Dragoons will follow when
equipt; at present they want every thing on the
face of the earth, so that with the scanty supply of
cash which you know the old Congress has been
carrying on their operations for these two years
with, we have no room to expect them shortly.
The Dutch have closed with the British respecting

Hostilities, this will cut out some work for enemy and very little helps—I was favoured with yours in Answer to mine concerning the officers Memorial. I have heard nothing of this affair from the first of it—I think it was impolitick at this day and may be attended with circumstances that will prejudice the service. I at first blamed you for it, but have since been informed from whence it originated, and therefore beg your pardon for entertaining a thought of the kind.

I am D.ʳ Capt.

With esteem

Yr. ob servt.

G. WEEDON.

WEEDON TO LIEUT. COL. JOHN F. MERCER.*

FREDKS., March 18th, 1783.

My dear Mercer:

I am honored by last nights post with your fav. 11th inst. It is pleasing tho' not conclusive as to the grand point, however one week more will no doubt clear up all our doubts & fears. Colo. Temple who left Phila. after the post is now with me, he assures me Capt. Barney has arrived with official Dispatches from our Ministers but cannot

*This letter and those which follow from Genl. Weedon were written when Col. Mercer was a Delegate from Virginia in the Continental Congress.

positively say what they are. One thing however gives me hopes they are such as we wish, and that is, we are scarcely one hour without private expresses from the Northern Min'trs to their Tobacco Agents in Virga. It therefore behoves you as a friend to the honest part of your country to communicate with Expedition the Glad tidings, when you are sufficiently informed & authorised so to do; be assured such Intelligence as you would wish should go abroad, shall have the first Circulation after it arrives to me. This little City affords not a syllable of any thing interesting or would informe you of it. I shall wait with patients for your next favr. and how will it elevate me to be informed of Peace.

I am my dear Colo. with sentiments of great esteem

& Regd. yr. obt. servt.

G. WEEDON.

WEEDON TO MERCER.

FREDERICKSBURG, Apl. 1st 1783.

My dear Colo:

Yours of the 24th Inst. per Express has opened all our Eyes. I cannot describe my feelings to You, nor is it possible for me to express the joy of Your Friends on this most Glorious and important event. I hope on this Occasion America will hold

in Eternal remembrance the good offices and bene-
fits she has recd. from our great and good ally—
she surely merits every thing we can do consistant
with the Dignity and Interest of our own Country.

Nothing rejoyces me more than to hear the dis-
turbances in the Army are reconciled, it would
have been a sad stain in the History of the war had
they gone to extremes, the Liberal allowance of
Congress in lue of half pay must give general satisfaction and will enable we poor Continentals to.
drink our Beer with a contented mind.

This place affords nothing new. Your Brother
James just had time to Drink a *Peace* Bowl with
me before he set out for Richmond, he took his
departure last Sunday morning, fatter and more
cheerful than I ever saw him. All other friends
are well.

I am Dr. Colo. with real affection, Yr. obt servt.

G. WEEDON.

WEEDON TO MERCER.

FREDERICKSBURG, May 20th 1783.

Dear Colo:

I am honored with your 13th Inst. which has
almost given me a fever; by your information I
conclude public Debts will remain Public Debts,
for some time, which by no means suits my Finances, as I never wish to become a Creditor in

the Funds, with not a shilling to go to market with. We are told here of three months pay to be immediately advanced the Army; do confirm this account, and call on me for a bottle of wine when ever you please. A very full meeting of the Officers of the Virg^a line was held here on Monday the 12th Inst. when the sense of the Gentlemen was collected respecting the Resolutions of Congress 23d of March. They were unanimous in accepting the commutation in lue of half pay on the terms offered, when ever disbanded by Authority.

We already begin to taste the blessings of Peace. Our Rivers feel the weight of Foreign burthens, which the Assembly have admitted to an entrance as their first measure this session. Goods have fallen nearly to old price. Tobacco in a general way 20/. but believe 22/6 has been given. Wheat 21/. & Corn 15/. the latter rising fast and will be 20/. in this place e'er long. This article I have to buy, and none of the others to sell. Your Brother dined with me yesterday, he is as hearty as a buck, as are all your other Friends. Fitzhugh is in Richmond. Madam is about the size of Miss Peggy M—. I think she is pretty sure of a brace at least. Do transmit the paymasters account so soon as You are able to procure it, and tell me how the evacuation of N. Y. goes on, and what the result of the conference between the two great Military Characters, when the Army is likely to be disbanded, and whether any will be retained in service.

> I am with real Esteem
> > Yr obt. servt.
> > > G. WEEDON.

WEEDON TO MERCER.

FREDERICKSBURG, Sept. 9th 83.

My dear Colo:

You are at least two letters Indebted to me, and from never writing any of Your old Friends I believe in my Conscience you have forgot us all. I hear you have been long indisposed, let me enquire now after your health. I observe You are now Arranging Your Peace Establishment which will require deep and serious Deliberations, but having the Aid of His Excellency have not a doubt but all will be right. I was thinking that an officer in each State should be retained in service as an Adjutant Genl. whose Business it should be not only to Inspect the Militia of the State but also the Post and Magazines and to make Report thereof every Quarter or half Year. No doubt however but the General will think of every thing proper, and if any snugg post or place in the Peace Establishment should offer where I can be of service You will particularly oblige me in proposing me. I am rather of the rong side of life to look far forward in

Business and wish to be employ'd the remainder of my days in some way that I am more acquainted with.

I have not any News worth communicating. Your Brothers are boath well as are all Your other Friends. I wish You could be hear the first of next month to purtake of our Races, but Your moments are more advantageously employ'd. I shall bring Billy Mercer to Phila. in October, and perhaps may have the pleasure of seeing you.

I am Very affectionately Yr. obt servt.

G. WEEDON.

WEEDON TO MERCER.

FREDERICKSBURG, Octobr 12th, 1783.

I am to thank you my Dear Colo. for the Friendship Expressed in Your last fav. wch. I had the honor to receive by post. Not having anything worth communicating at that time, deferred acknowledging the Rect. till this week in hopes of picking up something that might amuse for a few minutes. It would be laughable enough for me to touch on foreign affairs when You are so much better informed in point of Intelligence, Domestic matters must therefore be the resource to apply to. Our Races are over, and I know it matters very little with you who won, or who lost; so it does with me, but my three Guineas are gone never

more to return. Farmer Selden carried the Beef
premium hollow, not a little pleased as You may
suppose, and besides the Bounty the old fellow
touched 19d. pr. pound for the Carcass, indeed it
was by far the best meat I ever saw, and of the
white back bread. The Races lasted three Days
and brought together more people by two thirds
than I ever remember to have seen on any similar
occation. As to ladies they were not to be num-
bered. Balls every night ; but I know this amuse-
ment dont hit your fancy either, for I well remember the last I had the pleasure of seeing you at
[a ball] you complained of it's being the only im-
prudent step you could charge yourself with in
life: however it may not be unpleasant to inform
your sisters were all so well as to take a part in the
Dances. Mrs. Garnot made one of the party.
Among other thing we had a General Meeting of
the *Cloath*, such as it now is. Necessity however
has no law, the Back is nothing, the Heart is all
and I can venture to say a truer band never pistle
cocked. Do my Dear Colo. inform me immediately
the situation of our land Business. I understand
Congress have accepted the Cession of Virga. but
would be glad to know whether in doing this, they
have considered the prayer of our Petition to the
last Assembly in which we solicit a part of the
lands that they had oferred to Congress laying between the little and great Miami's.

I am very desirous of being fully advised in this matter, to prevent as far as lays in my power the poor officers from parting with their Warrants, which they are now disposing of for a song, not knowing where they are to be located. I am sure You will find leisure to communicate anything that tends to the benefit of Your Field companions and shall thank You to be as explicite as possible for their information. We are in hopes of fixing everything this session of Assembly and to know clearly on what ground we stand. I have twice hinted to you the propriety of your Claim, with an offer of attending to it, but have never received a line from you respecting the matter, which needs no further explanation than what I have in my previous letters suggested, and can only add that I am still at Your service should You chose to offer Your pretentions which I cant but think are just.

I am with every sentiment of esteem

Your obt servt.

G. WEEDON.

THE SCUDDER AFFAIR.*

* " Scudder v. Gray, Claimant. Appeal from a judgment in
the County Court of Fairfield County, Connecticut, May 31,
1779, lodged with the Committee on Appeals, December 23,
1780, reversed by the Court of Appeals."—See Vol. 131, U. S.
Reports, p. xlii of Appendix.

The statement of the case as it appears in the U. S. Supreme
Court Archives shows that William Smith Scudder, owner of the
sloop *Ranger*, with a crew of nine men, was commissioned by
Governor Clinton as a privateersman with power to seize and
make prize of all goods, shipping, merchandize and effects liable
to confiscation. He went in pursuance of this commission into
Long Island Sound, and on December 20th, 1778, landed at
Huntington, L. I,, within the enemy's lines, where he seized a
large quantity of goods and chattels, all, however, belonging to
British subjects. Washington's orders to Col. Gray had been
positive. He was to permit no one to pass to Long Island, except for the purpose of gaining necessary military intelligence,
and in no case was any plundering of the inhabitants, Whig or
Tory, to be permitted. Gray exacted a promise from Scudder
to cruise only in the Sound, and on this understanding permitted
him to pass the guards, and after Scudder had made his seizures
Gray took all the goods into his custody and reported his action
to his superior officers. The case having been brought before
the County Court was decided in Scudder's favor, probably on
the ground that he had molested none but Tories; but the Court
of Appeals reversed this decision and condemned the seized
goods as lawful prize of the United States, compelling the libel-
lant, Scudder, to pay the costs of the suit.

GENERAL PARSONS TO MAJOR GRAY.*

20th Sept. 1778.

Sir:

Before a Post was established at Norwalk, the General order'd Lt. Brewster to that Place with Directions to ingage a Number of Men, Refugees or others to keep up a Communication with Long Island & New York to gain Intelligence, this they did untill the Post was establish'd and you ordered to command, on which the whole Government & Direction of that matter of course devolv'd upon you, and it is undoubtedly your Duty to prevent any Irregularities by those of the Army or Country whereby the Ends you are design^d to answer may be frustrated, and no Person can have Right to pass over to the Island from your Post on any Pretence but by your consent unless by order of the Commander in Chief or other your Superior officer; nor can any prior order of the General warrant their passing after you was sent to this command.

Yr. ob. serv.

SAML. H. PARSONS.

GENERAL WASHINGTON TO LIEUT. COL. GRAY.

HEADQUARTERS FREDERICKSBURG, 31st Octobr, 1778.

Sir:

It has been intimated to me that several persons

---

* Ebenezer Grey was commissioned Lieut. Col. 6th Conn. Infty., October 15, 1778.

have gone over to Long Island, under the pretext of gaining intelligence, and indiscriminately distressed and plundered the inhabitants. As such a conduct is totally incompatible with obtaining information or making discoveries, I do not imagine you have given any sanction to such proceedings. But that so pernicious a practice may be the more effectually prevented—you will prevent any persons whatever from making excursions to the Island—and only employ those as spies or observers, in whom you can place a proper confidence.

I am Sir

Your most obed^t Servt

G. WASHINGTON.

GENERAL ISRAEL PUTNAM TO LIEUT. COL. GRAY.

HEAD QUARTERS, 2 Decr 1778.

Sir:

I have received your Letters of the 22^d Inst., enclosing a Copy of his Excellencys orders to you— I had before heard of the affair of Scudder, both from Genl Parsons & himself; I entirely approve of your Conduct, in taking the goods into your Custody, until some determination can be had concerning them, & would have you retain them till such Time—I have wrote to Genl Washington & Govr Clinton on the subject.

As to Rogers,* who was sent under guard, I cannot find, upon an examination of the Articles of War, that he is tryable by a Court Martial—but if he is, the crime should be made out particularly against him, & the evidence annex'd to it—I have therefore sent him back to be despos'd of as you think proper—& have to observe that if you are still of opinion, that there is such evidence against him, as that a Court Martial will take Cognizance of the matter he may be brought before it on Monday or Tuesday Next, at which Times a Court will set at this place; In order to this all the Evidence ought to be collected & digested in a proper manner.

The civil power is exceeding jealous lest the Military should make encroachments on its Jurisdiction, for which reason I could wish matters might not be drawn into question, where the Jurisdiction of Courts Martial, is not obvious ; we have had one instance, within these few days, where the Prisoners, tho' guilty of robbing the publick Stores, were not consider'd by the Court Martial as capable of being tryed by them—

I am Sir your humble serv^t .

ISRAEL PUTNAM.

---

* This is Jarvis Rodgers, evidently, who was one of Scudder's associates. A letter to him from Abigail Smith follows. Emmons' *United States Navy, from 1775 to 1853*, shows J. Rodgers, of Connecticut, captain privateer boat *Argo*, with a force of 15 men. The boat was captured eventually by the British.

PUTNAM TO GOV. CLINTON.*

Sir:

This Letter will be handed to your Excellency by Cap^n Wm Scudder who I understand has your Commission to cruize, under Colour of which I am further informed, he has within these few Days been on Long Island & brought off a quantity of Goods from thence—These Lt. Col. Gray who is stationed at Norwalk, has seiz'd and holds in his hands, untill some legal determination can be had on the matter.

The particulars of this affair, and the conduct of several other persons, Inhabitants of your State, will be reported to your Excellency by Brig^{dr} Genl. Parsons, who is entirely acquainted with the subject, and possessed of the original evidence concerning it.

As this is a matter, which falls under your immediate cognozance, I thought proper to make this representation of it,—and to inform you that the orders of the Commander in Chief are, that no kind of property be taken from any person, under pretense of its belonging to Tories—These orders I am determined shall be most particularly complied wth by the Troops under my command that every violation of them shall be severely Punished

---

*From the MS. copy in the Archives of the U. S. Supreme Court.

—Wth regard to others, who are not accountable to me for their conduct, I shall take no more upon myself, than to inform those to whom they are, of the Circumstances that the [sic] may be exculpated, and blame (if there be any) fall only where it is merited.

I have wrote to his Excellency, the Commander-in-Chief, Governor Trumbull on the abuses committed in the Sound on Long Island, should have troubled your Excellency on the same subject by the first opportunity had not this affair occurred.

As to Mr. Scudder personally, I know nothing to his disadvantage, but have heard that he is a brave man, has suffered much and done considerable service in the cause of his country. All that I wish is that justice may take place, to which I know you are equally disposed.

I am your Excellency's

Most obt. humbl. servt.

ISRAEL PUTNAM.

GOV. CLINTON TO GENERAL PUTNAM.*

POUGHKEEPSIE, Dec. 25, 1778.

Sir:

I am favoured with your letter of the 22d inst., by Capt. Scudder. I have always believed that

---

* From the MS. copy in the Archives of the U. S. Supreme Court.

Whigs on Long Island suffered indiscriminately wth the Tories from the Parties who have from time to time been on Long Island, owing to the villainy of some and indiscretion of other of them. From a conviction of this being the case, I have not in any Instance given my authority to any of these Parties. You may rest assured, Sir, that nothing will be done which may in the least interfere with the order of the Commander in Chief, but on the contrary you will meet with every aid in carrying them into execution. Cap^n Scudder I have reason to believe is a Brave, Honest man. His Comission authorizes him to cruize on the Sound only, & I doubt not but he will meet with every encouragement from you which can be Granted consistent with the good of the Public service.

I am,

Sir, with great Respect,

Your most obt. Servt.,

GEO. CLINTON.

GENERAL PARSONS TO LIEUT. COL. GRAY.

FAIRFIELD, 31 Decr 78.

Dr Colo:

Mr. Scudder has return^d from Gov^n Clinton; but no Decision is yet had on his Goods; Genl Putnam directs that every article which was sav^d be kept safe until further orders, and that you furnish

Scudder with a Copy of the Invoice of the Goods &c seisd if he requests it.

You will forward such evidence as you have or may receive concerning this excursion, as soon as you can to Genl. Putnam or me, the Particular Situation & number of the Troops at Oyster Bay is necessary to be known speedily. I wish [MS. torn] to take proper measures for [MS. torn] Purpose & inform. Yr ob serv

SAM.ᴸ H. PARSONS.

The boat you will deliver up and continue to prevent passing to Long Island.

S. PARSONS.

PUTNAM TO GRAY.

CAMP READING, Feby. 10ᵗʰ 1779.

Sir:

I am favor'd with your letter of yesterday's date, and am much oblig'd for the intelligence.

As Scudder has Governor Clintons Commission to Cruize on the Sound, I know not of any authority by which I can forbid him—however as you will know before this reaches you, what becomes of the Goods that was seized, so you will be better able to determine your line of conduct in future.— If it should not be given in Scudders favour, I would have you keep a look out & sieze him & every thing that he may bring off.

In the meantime I desire you will furnish me with all the papers & Evidences of which you are possess'd, respecting Scudders former Conduct, & that of taking the Goods which you siezed in particular, that I may lay the whole matter before the Commander in Chief for his further directions.

I am Sir

Your most obed.^t servt.

ISRAEL PUTNAM.

P. S. The Traveling is so exceeding bad at present that I cannot conveniently send for the Oysters which you was good enough to offer, but a few days will determine whether the Roads will be properly settled, or the Ground hard froze.

ABIGAIL SMITH TO JARVIS ROGERS.

HUNTINGTON [SUFFOLK CO., L. I.]
MARCH THE 12 [1779]

My dear Sir:

I am wonce moer a going to rit you a few lines in which I have the pleasure to let you to know that I am well and your fathers family is well But I must let you know that I have Reseived your agreeable letter to Day that you sent By Mr. talor But I should have been very happy to have received it Befoer to have sent won by him I have thought the time Long that I did not hear from you I did not think that the time wold have Ben

so long Before I see or heard from you but a this
unhappy war it seems as if their never wod be an
end to it for my part I am almost disspair of even
seeing any Beter teims but O my Dear Sir I must
Beg favour of you that you will rit to me and let
me know if you had your things taking from you
with the plundered goods but pray Dont never at-
temt to come on such a desin again if you have
any regard for me or your fathers family O did
you know what a trouble is to me to hear every
won a teling a Bout you plundering I am sur you
would Leave of the traid for I wold not do any
thing that wold lay you so much troubel pray remember me to my Brothers

this from yoer faithful friend

ABIGAIL SMITH

GENERAL ISRAEL PUTNAM.

HEAD QUARTERS, PEEKSKILL, 27 Sept., 1777.

Sir:

I have just Receiv'd, a Letter from General Washington* Dated 34 miles up Schuylkill wherein he informs me that Genl. Howes Army had found means to cross Schuylkill, several miles below his Army; upon which He has ordered a further reinforcement from this Post, of which

---

* The letter referred to is dated Sept. 23, 1777, and is as follows:

"*Dr Sir:*

"The situation of our affairs in this Quarter calls for every aid and for every effort. Gen'l Howe, by various manoeuvers and marching high up the Schuylkill, as if he meant to turn our Right Flank, found means by countermarching to pass the River several miles below us last night. * * * I therefore desire, that, without a moment's loss of time, you will detach as many effective rank and file under proper generals and other officers as will make the whole number, including those with Genl McDougall, amount to twenty-five hundred privates & non-commissioned fit for duty. * * * * * That you may not hesitate about complying with this order, you are to consider it as peremptory & not to be dispensed with. Colonel Malcom's regiment will form a part of the detachment." Ford's *Writings of Washington* Vol. 6, p. 84.

corps you must join. You will therefore upon the rec[t]. of this prepare to join Genl. Parsons Brigade, whom I have ordered up from the White Plains. I shall endeavor to send some militia to guard the stores Remaining in the Clave. Your Baggage must go with you.

> I am Sir
> Your very
> Hble sev[t]
> ISRAEL PUTNAM, M. G.

To Colonel Malcom.

JOHN PAUL JONES.

JONES TO JONATHAN WILLIAMS.[*]

BREST, Novr 5th, 1778.[†]

I had the pleasure of writing you, my dear sir, the 31st ult., inclosing a Bill of Lading for 15 Hh^{ds} of Porter, and I believe it will not be amiss to reserve one of them for me, as it is highly probable that I may this Winter fit out at or near Nantes if a suitable ship can be found. I have at last found means to purchase, and should be glad to hear of a very fast sailing Frigate of from 36 to 40 Guns. I impatiently wait the result of your inquiries in consequence of my last.

I thank you for your favor of 27th ulto. You lay before me circumstances which can be best seen thro' by the candid eye of Friendship, whose councils always merit attention. I am not ill pleased that you can discover a species of inflexibility in my nature which will not suffer me to kneel at the feet of haughty Power, or to stoop where I cannot

---

[*] A nephew of Benjamin Franklin, and agent at Nantes for the American commissioners at Paris.

[†] Jones was busy at this time trying to obtain a suitable frigate in France. A little later he procured his famous ship, "Le Bon Homme Richard."

also Esteem. I know that this turn of mind is highly unfavorable to any who would obtain court favor or promotion in Europe; yet I find no inclination to alter my disposition. And tho in my life I have met with some severe Trials, if I cannot rise by even and direct dealing, I will not rise at all.

I would have sent you the inclosed letter of Attorney by the last Post—but I thought a witness necessary to prove it in Nantes, and was unsuccessfully employed in looking after a person for that purpose untill it was too late.

With respect to my 3/20^{ths} of the Drake—I think you need only represent that I still hold my share and that you agree to this as the purchaser of the 17/20^{ths}—the matter of Commission will thus be out of the Question—the affair will remain between you and me, and I promise you that I shall make no sort of difficulty about its settlement.

As to the affair of the Countess of Selkirks Plate, it is deposited in the Kings Store, and I am ready to account for the Captors part to any person who proves himself properly authorized.—Tho' perhaps it may be found more properly to be my own province to remit the amount to the Captain in articles that will sell at an high advance in America.

I am with sincere affection
Your obliged Friend & Servant
Jno P. Jones.

Jonathan Williams, Esq.

DR. SAMUEL TENNEY.

DANBURY (CONNT.) November 29, 1779.

Dear Sir:

When I inform you that I am in a cold fireless chamber, writing on a Tea table so completely in Ruins, that it is with the utmost Difficulty I can, with two Knees & one Hand keep it together, you will have a more convincing Proof of my warm Friendship for you & your agreeable & amiable Lady, than the most specious Protestations could possibly afford. Till I met with Col. Folsom, in this place, two Days since, I had never heard from you nor a single Friend in Exeter since I parted with them. By your own Feelings on similar Occasions, you may judge of the Happiness I enjoyed in hearing by him of your Welfare.

Soon after I left Exeter, I joined my Regiment at Rhode Island, found my Friends well, & have spent the time very happily until since the evacuation of Newport. We are now on our Way to Head-Quarters, which is to be near Morristown in

---

* Dr Samuel Tenney was a Surgeon in the New Hampshire line, and was cousin to Hon. Joseph Gilman.

N. Jersey. Our Unhappiness now is that we have to build our own winter Quarters, at a Time when we ought to be in them; and after a Summer of Idleness & Luxury, to spend the Winter in Penury & Fatigue. But upon every Adversity in a military Life, the Frenchman says, *C'est la Fortune de Guerre*, & makes himself easy;—& I know of no better Way than to imitate him. He is certainly happy who is contented with his situation.

Had the British Army, & consequently our Regiment, continued at Rhode Island, I pleas'd myself with the Thoughts of spending some Part of the Winter with my Friends at Exeter & elsewhere—but now the Distance will be so greatly increas'd that I am uncertain whether so much Happiness will fall to my Share.

But, be that as it may, neither Distance nor Time will ever be able to efface or diminish those warm Sentiments of Respect & Esteem with which I have the Honor to,

   my Dear Sir,
    Yours & Mrs. Gilman's
     Very sincere Friend
      & most obt Servt
       SAMˡ TENNEY.

Mr. Joseph Gilman.

CAPTAIN WILLIAM BEATTY.

BEATTY TO GOVERNOR THOMAS S. LEE.*

FREDᵏ TOWN, March 9th 80.

Sir:

It is with pleasure that I can inform your Excellency that my success in the recruiting service obliges me to call on you for two Thousand Dollars, or an order for that sum. I have enclos'd an account of the money I receiv'd last by which you will find the number of men I have Inlisted. I am under the necessity of sending my recruits to Camp without Coats, vests or overalls, as the cloathing expected from Baltimore has never arrived. The recruits Cant be Conveniently kept here any longer. My Being on this Command deprives me of Every opportunity of drawing the stores allow'd by the state, which I am under the greatest necessity for.

---

* William Beatty was captain in Col. Gemby's 1st Maryland Regt. which "gained the battle of Cowpens and were preëminently distinguished in the retreat through North Carolina and at the battle of Guilford" (Marshall's *Washington*.) Young Beatty distinguished himself by his bravery, and, at the battle of Hobkirk's Hill, 25th April, 1780, received a wound from which he died, in the 23d year of his age. See "A New Biographical Dictionary and Remembrancer" (1824). Thos. S. Lee was at this time governor of Maryland.

I should be glad your Excellency would allow me the priviledge of purchasing the stores due me according to the Act of Assembly, or authorize some person to furnish me with them.

Mr Thos Beatty, the Bearer hereof, promises to bring me Cash or Order.

I am your Excellencies

Most obt Hubl servt,

W. BEATTY.

GENERAL DAVID COBB.

COBB * TO COL. HENRY JACKSON.

BOSTON, 8th June, 1780.

My dear Colo :

I wrote you by the last post, & received yours by Bright—You can't conceive what an uproar Rivington's paper from New York† has put this Town into; the Dog has publish'd an account of the surrendery of Charlestown on the 12th ult., but from the manner of his relating the matter & some other circumstances, added to his being the damn'd-est lyar in the World, makes a number of us disbelieve it, tho' the greatest part of the Town are in full faith—The Government, in consequence of

---

* David Cobb had served in Rhode Island and New Jersey in 1777–1778 as Lieutenant-colonel in Henry Jackson's regiment. He was for several years Aide-de-camp to General Washington, and at the close of the war had risen to the rank of Colonel and Brevet Brigadier General.

† James Rivington published till the end of the war, "The New York Gazetteer; or the Connecticut, New Jersey, Hudson's River, and Quebec Weekly Advertiser." He "offended even his own party by the gross fabrications which appeared in his columns, and was repeatedly obliged to apologize. The paper went by the name of the Lying Gazette."—*Magazine of American History;* Feby., 1887. On this occasion, however, Rivington spoke the truth.

orders from Congress, have assest 4000 men to be rais'd immediately to fill their Battalions, they are engag'd for six months. As this will supercede at present, any occasion for Recruiting officers, I think it best, in the course of a fortnight, to order on all ours that are here.—I have applied to some members of Council about recruiting Money, they tell me that they have appropriated a Large Sum for that purpose, which is now with Genl. Patterson at West point; you may get what sum you please by sending to him—the money for your private purse, I must wait your orders respecting the notes.—Two Lads Lowell, a deserter reinlisted for War, & Thos. Elliot who I took for Jones, have gone on—do write me who of the Regt. are still absent, I know of none of the war men on furlough that have deserted,—old Nelson told me that Blanchard had deserted into the Coos Country, where, he says, numbers of deserters are gone to settle some wild Lands. I am sorry you returned Cottell & Giggett deserted, as I am very certain they never meant to leave the| Regt—their Ignorance has lead 'em into the error, they are two fine armorers & would be a loss to the Regt.; I'll send em directly—Renopt will be on soon—old Waltt & Stutering Bob are still here—I'd have you and your officers exercise every kind of Lenity to the Soldiers that is consistent with Discipline, as you'll thereby endear the soldiery to you and in-

duce numbers to return with pleasure from deser-
tion to service under you; it will likewise take off
that curse of slander that is now pervading all the
Country Towns in this Government, that the Continental officers are so cruel and severe that the
men can never be got to serve under 'em; and you
may be assur'd that the Leading members of the
House meet with the greatest difficulty in getting
a majority of the Country members to assent that
the 4000 men now raising should serve under Continental officers, so great is the prejudice.—You
can't meet a man of any Influence from the
Country, but he'll tell you that they never shall be
able to raise their men unless they appoint their
officers, for the men, they say, will never serve
under Continental officers, because they have been
to badly treated by 'em; so great is the Ignorance
of this sett of people that they eagerly swallow any
malicious slander that any villinous soldier may
propigate against the best character in the Army;
this is a prejudice that must be combated with all
the force of art and Intrigue, for I conceive that
this will have the most fatal tendency to the op-
position of this Country, of anything that has
happened during the contest. We have a report
here that the Massachusetts Line are to be reduc'd
to 10 Regts. & the 10 oldest Cols. command them
& whatever officers that are supernumerary to retire on half pay &c. Do inform of the truth of this;

for I do assure you that I have no fancy at present of serving in a different corps than what I have heretofore serv'd in; you know that if this new arrangement takes place (which I conceive to be perfectly right) I shall be chas'd into some other Reg^t that will make me very unhappy & consequently defeat all my pleasure, as it is from the agreeableness of connection that I continu'd in service—You'll write every post,—let me know your wishes respecting my stay here—if the French Fleet arrives I shall be on without *invitation*, if it dont I shall be at your command—my Love to the Maj^r & officers—my best respect to Gen^ls Green & Knox and accept the warmest wishes for your happiness from your friend.

DAVID COBB.

Col. Henry Jackson.

COL. ALEXANDER SCAMMELL.

June 9, 1781.

. . . . . I am confident you have not been wanting in your exertions for us. Our soldiers—poor fellows, I feel distressed for them beyond description—they are ragged, very ragged, but a small degree removed from stark nakedness. I would suppose that our brother citizens are doing everything in their power for us, while we are enjoying Continental fare in the field. Their political salvation depends on a good army well found. I shudder at the prospect of the ensuing campaign, not from fear of the enemy, but from apprehensions of starvation. The supplies are so very precarious that the Commander-in-Chief cannot lay a single plan nor commence a single operation, for want of the necessary supplies. What a pity that our great and good General should be cramped in his operations, which, perhaps, if well seconded, might this

---

*Alexander Scammell was Colonel of the 3ᵈ New Hampshire Regt. from 1776 to 1780 and served as Adjutant General of the Continental army. The above letter was written from the South to Hon. Joseph Gilman, Chairman of Committee of Safety of New Hampshire.

campaign be decisive! I wright this part only for our stanch Whigg friends. I don't wish the Tories might know the circumstances, least they should triumph. Make use of it as a Spurr at our Assembly, as many of them as you can trust . . . . .

NICHOLAS GILMAN.

GILMAN* TO COL. RICHARD VARRICK.

TEAN NECK, August 28th '80.

Dear Sir:

I have to acknowledge the rect of yours of the 25th by Express—but am unhappy, that several circumstances are so obstinately combined to counteract my wishes and disappoint your expectations. A long and tedious servitude in the Orderly Office, a continual round of the same mechanical business, and many other considerations, has rendered the duties of the office disagreeable in a high degree; that I should be pleased with the idea of serving General Arnold provided my appointment could be a positive one, and the General should

---

* Nicholas Gilman was at 21 Adjutant of Colonel Alexander Scammell's regiment of the New Hampshire line, and in 1778 was promoted to Captain, and was Deputy Adjutant-General to take account of the prisoners captured upon the surrender of Lord Cornwallis at Yorktown. He was a member of Congress for New Hampshire 1786–1788, also member of the Convention which met at Philadelphia, 1787, to frame a Constitution. He was member of Congress from New Hampshire 1789–1797, and in 1805 he was Senator from New Hampshire and served until the day of his death, May 2, 1814. In 1780 he was urged by Major-General Arnold to accept an appointment under him, but he declined.—See Appleton's *Cyclopædia of American Biography.*

(154)

find himself able to command in the field—the latter objection in this critical State of affairs has great weight—If I should come into your family and be confined in the dreary wilderness of the highlands while our operations are going on against the City, which possibly may be the case, my situation would be as distressing as that of Fabius M. when he had recourse to the flaming cattle.

As matters have gone I am sorry the appointment was offered me, as I fear it has prevented the Generals applying to another person and think you must be in great want of assistance.

If I can render you any service in my present station, shall be happy to do it, as I think to continue here a few months longer, and then to seek a new mode of life.

Be pleased to make my Compts to Majr Franks,
   & believe me to be with sincere regard
     Dear Sir
       Your most obt Servant
         N. GILMAN.

Col. Richard Varrick
   Secy to M. General Arnold
     Robinson House.

GILMAN TO HON. JOSEPH GILMAN.

PHILADELPHIA, September 18, 1787.

Dear Sir:

The important business of the Convention being closed, the Secretary set off this morning to present Congress with a report of their proceedings, which I hope will come before the States in the manner directed, but as some time must necessarily elapse before that can take place, I do myself the pleasure to transmit the enclosed papers for your private satisfaction forbearing all comments on the plan but that it is the best that could meet the unanimous concurrence of the States in Convention; it was done by bargain and Compromise, yet notwithstanding its imperfections, on the adoption of it depends (in my feeble judgment) whether we shall become a respectable nation, or a people torn to pieces by intestine commotions, and rendered contemptible for ages.

Please present my most respectful regards to Mrs. Gilman, my love to my friend Tenny & Cousin Ben, of whose return I was very glad to hear.

I am with the greatest Respect

Dr Sir

Your most Obedient and

Humble Servant,

NICH. GILMAN.

Hon'ble Joseph Gilman, Esqr.

BARON STEUBEN.

STEUBEN TO COL. MEADE.*

June 30, 1781.

My dear Meade:

Your letter handed by the express I have this moment received. To-morrow I set out for Charlottesville,† consequently shall have no occasion for the lads you were so good as to send me. As it is of the greatest moment that the Marquis

---

* Col. Meade was on Steuben's staff.

† Steuben had experienced so much difficulty in getting an effective force of men in Virginia, or any supplies for the few he was able to collect, that he was almost in despair. On 3^{d} June, 1781, he wrote Lafayette from Point of Fork : "Here I am with five hundred and fifty men in a desert, without shoes, shirts, and what is still worse, without cartridge-boxes. I write everywhere, send expresses to all parts of the world, but I receive no answer. If I did not expect Lawson, with a reinforcement, I would go to Charlottesville to Sing a jeremiad to my sovereign masters. Please let me have news from you. I am here as I would be in Kamschatka ; I do not know where you are, nor what has become of Cornwallis." In a very few days he was nearly surrounded by the enemy, and was obliged to make a hasty retreat into North Carolina, but in the latter part of June rejoined Lafayette. He then fell sick, and retired to a country place near Charlottesville where he remained until September.—Kapp's *Life of Steuben.* Compare also Steuben to Morgan, p. 15.

should be informed of the movements of the enemy
on the S? Side James River, (if they make any)
I think you can do no greater service than to proceed as low down on that side to be opposite their
fleet, & to be in continual correspondence with the
Marquis; from your knowledge & fidelity he will
be informed of everything, as it is, which will enable him to act with certainty.

The two expresses I send back. They may be
employed by you very beneficially. Was I to remain with the Army I would even then give up
the pleasure of seeing you and the benefit which I
have reason to expect from your advice & assistance; that you might undertake the above necessary business.

The Continental Line of the Army lay near the
bird ordinary, the militia at this place ab? 7 miles
above the bird—The British are 2 miles below the
town of Wilsbg At present we can form no con-
jecture of their intentions. With real esteem I am
Dear Meade your friend

and Humbl Servt
STEUBEN.

STEUBEN TO COLONEL WILLIAM DAVIE.*
NEAR CHARLOTTESVILLE, 27 July [1781].

Sir:

Capt Morrow with 56 horses belonging to Col.

* He was on Steuben's staff.

Washington's regiment is here without forage or provisions If there is a place fixed for the rendezvous of the cavalry I beg you to inform Capt. Morrow of it, through Col. Febiger or Maj Call. If there is no place yet pointed out I beg you to consult with Government on the matter; in the mean time Capt Morrow thinks Culpepper Co house will be the best place for the party to proceed to, not only on account of provisions & forage but the conveniency of artifficers by whom his equipage may be repaired. When the plan for the general rendezvous for the Cavalry is made the horse may then be drawn together

I am Sir

Your most Humbl St.

STEUBEN

Maj. Genl.

GENERAL JOHN BURGOYNE.

BURGOYNE TO ———

Au quartier général à Skenesborough, le 18 de
Juillet 1777.*

Monsieur:

Je vous prie de me pardonner d'avoir reçu deux
lettres de votre part sans faire réponse par écrit,
ayant été extrêmement occupé en finissant mes dé-
pêches à la cour.

Votre projet pour faire un mouvement de votre
Corps est fort à mon gré, & marque, dans toutes
ses parties, les titres que vous possédez. Les cir-
constances du tems cependant, m'empêchent d'en
profiter sans courir risque de trop fatiguer vos
troupes.

Il sera nécessaire de faire un mouvement en
avant avec toute l'armée aussi tôt que possible;
Je n'attend que d'avoir les chemins en état.

Je vous supplie de faire en sorte que l'esprit de
l'ordre par rapport à le renvoye des baggages des
officiers à Ticonderoga ayet (?) bien. Les baggages des officiers P——— sont déjà renvoyés et il
n'en reste à plusieurs qu'une petite trunk & une
valise. C'est réelment pour l'mbort (?) de l'officier
à la fin, que Je suis si porté à cet article.

---

* This was about three mouths before his surrender.

J'ai ordonné la distribution des cheveaux pour l'artillerie; après ce, ceux qui restent seront partegés parmi les troupes, mais jusqu'à présent il n'y a certes pas un nombre suffisant pour porter les tentes des soldats.

Les habitans de votre voisinage en excuse de n'avoir les enemi tiens (?) battaille, prétendant que le sorte (?) est employé pour le service de votre corps. Je vous serais fort obligé par un rapport du nombre des boeufs, chevaux, et charettes réelment employé, le régiment différence compris, afin que Je puisse corriger les habitans en ce que le pretexte est.

Ou travaille à présent pour méthodiser les nouveaux corps des Provinciaux. Il est nécessaire que Monsieur Sherwood retourne au plûtôt avec une partie de son monde pour avoir leurs noms enrôlés, & les autres officiers leurs régimens.

J'ai ordonné 4 dozain de vin de Port, & la même quantité de vin de Madeira de vous être envoyé. Je suis tres mortifié que l'état présent de ma caisse ne me permet pas de vous suppléer en plus grande quantité & de meilleurs sortes.

J'ai l'honneur d'être avec tous les sentimens de respect & 'attachement possible.

Monsieur

Votre tres Humble

& tres obéissant serviteur

J. BURGOYNE.

BURGOYNE TO MISS CAULFIELD.*

My dearest Sue:

I did not intend to write to-day, nor can I exceed one short paragraph, in consequence of one expression of yours of yesterday, and another in a letter of Lord D——. You seem to think the approbation of the Toilet was not sincere. He in a letter to me is quite in rapture of approbation on Miss F's opinion and his own.

I thought it absolutely necessary to tell you this to tune your song at your work; make all possible despatch, use all economy; if we must have four boxes, I should think the front and two ends wont be sufficient and the back saved, if the expense is of consequence.

I have sent you a pheasant and a brace of Partriges—both will keep, but particularly for a week if you chuse it. I give you the particulars, though at the loss of your indulgence in the curiosity of *rummaging*, because I find there is a practice in fashion of stealing half out of bushels of game.

Yours ever faithfully,

J. B.

Friday.

---

*Burgoyne married Lady Charlotte, youngest daughter of Lord Derby; she had died in 1776. It was after his return to England from America that he formed a connection with Susan Caulfield, a singer of some prominence, and by her he had three children, the eldest of whom was Sir John, who became a field marshal.

P. S.: Fie! Fie! to get such colds and pains in the stomach by feasting. If you did but take such care as I do!

GENERAL GEORGE WASHINGTON.

No. 3000.

TO LIEUT. COLONEL ROBERT HANSON HARRISON, ESQ.

Lieut. Colonel in the Continental Army; entered the service in the month of October 1775 as one of my Aid-de-Camp, and in May following became my Secretary. The duties of which office he discharged with Conspicuous abilities. That his whole conduct during all the interesting period of the War has been marked by the strictest integrity and the most attentive and faithful service, while by personal bravery he has been distinguished on many occasions.

Given at my head quarters this Twenty-fifth day of March 1781.

G.º WASHINGTON.

GENERAL WASHINGTON TO GEORGE STEPTOE WASHINGTON.*

NEWBURGH, Aug. 18th, 1783.

Dear George:

If my letter from Albany by the Count de Vienne has reached you, it would inform you that I had

---

* The General's nephew.

just made the tour of the Northern and Western parts of this State, & had got that far on my return home.—Accordingly the day following I Arrived at this place & found your Aunt but just recovering from a Fever and severe Cholic, which had reduced her much.—Since that she has had a relapse, and is at this Moment far from being in a good state of health.—

It gave us much concern to hear by Col̲o̲ Cobb that you had been very unwel, altho' better when he left you—I would Advise you to persevere in a temperate mode of living & give the climate a fair chance.—Too much retirement may be as improper as to be always in a crowd—extremes should be avoided.—If you want anything let me know it.—

Congress having required my attendance, I shall set off for Princeton to-morrow, and it is not likely that I shall return to this Quarter again, to reside. I carry my Baggage with me, it being the desire of Congress that I should remain there till the Arrival of the Definitive Treaty which as for the three last months is every day expected.—The British seem to be more in earnest to evacuate New York than heretofore, otherwise things in this quarter remain in statu quo.

Our best wishes attend you.

I am yours affect̲l̲

G̲o̲ WASHINGTON.

INVITATION TO DINNER.

General & Mrs. Washington present their compliments to Mr. And^{r.} Ramsay, Mrs. Ramsay, and Mr. Willm. Ramsay, and request the favour of their company to dine on Tuesday next, with the couple newly married.*

Mount Vernon,

23^{d.} Feb., 1799.

An answer is requested.

M^{R.} AND^{R.} RAMSAY, &C.,

in

Alexandria.

WASHINGTON TO MARTIN COCKBURN. †

Mount Vernon, May 3^{d.}, 1786.

Sir:

Being informed that you receive the lists of taxable property in Truro Parish, I do, tho. late, send you that of mine.

Do you hire your negro Tailor by the year?   If

------

* Mr. and Mrs. Lawrence Lewis. Eleanor Parke Custis, Mrs. Washington's grand-daughter, was married to Genl. Washington's nephew, Lawrence Lewis, Feb'y 22, 1799.

† Martin Cockburn, Esq., was a neighbor of Washington's, living at "Springfield," adjoining "Gunston Hall" and "Lexington," Va.

so on what terms and is, he now, or will he soon be disengaged?

My compliments, in which Mrs. Washington joins me, are offered to Mrs. Cockburn.

I am, Sir,

Yr. most obdt. servt,

Go. WASHINGTON.

GEORGE AUGUSTINE WASHINGTON.

GEORGE A. WASHINGTON* TO COL. JOHN F. MERCER.

MOUNT VERNON, May 24th, 1789.

Dear Sir:

I have received your favor of the 22d Inst., and with it was delivered by your Servant ninety-four pounds ten Shillings and seven pence half penny Verginia Currency for the President, which sum shall be passed to your credit. You mentioned having forwarded Bill No. 4 to him. Bills No. 2 & 3 which I rec'd, will be retained for his directions, and so soon as I am advised, you shall be informed the result.

Be pleased to present Mrs. Washington's Compliments to Mrs. Mercer with mine.

I am Dear Sir with much esteem,
Your most Obt Ser.
GEO. A. WASHINGTON.

GEO. A. WASHINGTON TO MERCER.

MOUNT VERNON, Decr 17th, 1789.

Dear Sir:

Your Favor which was dated shortly after I

---

* Major George A. Washington was General Washington's nephew, and attended to the affairs of Mt. Vernon.

parted with you at Fredericksburg met with some
delay in getting to me. The President has been
informed of the contents, and in reply says, as an
act of Providence has interposed to render a
complyance with your promise impracticable, he
must have further patience. He has also been
consulted as you desired, to know if wheat would
be received in payment. Clean & sound wheat
will be taken at his Mill and the Alexandria
Cash price allowed for it. The Crop of Corn
made here this year will be inadequate to the
demands, will therefore be glad to be informed
on the rec.t of this if you will have any to dispose of and on what terms you will engage to
deliver it here, or have it taken from your landing.
Mrs. Washington joins me in best respects to Mrs.
Mercer.

I am Dear Sir Your most obt. ser.

GEO. A. WASHINGTON.

GEO. A. WASHINGTON TO MERCER.

MOUNT VERNON, May 19th, 1791.

Dear Sir:

I had for some time been expecting the draught
you thought you would be able to give me on Alexandria, when I received your Letter, desiring I
would draw on you for eight hundred Dollars, but
it being without date of place or time and not hav-

ing come to hand long since, I was at a loss where
to direct, but imagine from the tenor of your Letter that you would be at Annapolis, and was writing to you at that place, when it was confirmed by
your letter of the 5th inst. dated there. I expected
you would have forwarded the money you have for
the President to this place, but being extremely
pressed for money went to Alexandria to endeavour
to accomodate you by getting some one to take a
draught on Annapolis, but could meet with no
person who had transactions in that place that
would enable them to do it, but meeting with Mr.
Fendall who was going there I will cheerfully
risque any sum you may pay to him on the President's Acct. I have therefore drawn on you for
the eight hundred Dollars your first Letter authorised me to do, and as you speak of a considerable
sum have desired him to receive, and pass a receipt
which shall be good against the president for any
further sum you may choose to forward. The two
statements I rec:d under cover from you at Fredericksburg I shewd the president, but his stay being
short at Mount Vernon he did not go into an examination of them, but observed to me that all he
wished was a just settlement and that he had long
been desirous of bringing the business to a close,
and should any difficulty attend it there will on
the part of the president be no objection to having
the accts. examined and settled by persons quali-

fied to do it, and that it is his wish that the business should be closed with mutual satisfaction I have no doubt.

      I am

         Dear Sir with esteem

             Your obt. Sev.

                 G̥o A. WASHINGTON.

Colo. John F. Mercer.

AARON OGDEN.

AARON OGDEN TO HIS WIFE.

WASHINGTON, April 26, 1802.*

My very dear Wife:

Yesterday, being Sunday, was spent at Mount Vernon, whereby I was prevented from writing to you, in my usual [sic].

The visit was very agreeable, and interested my feelings exceedingly. The prospects are fine, and the grounds, which are laid out, very extensive— the whole in a style very grand indeed—it appears, like works of its once Great possessor, and is a style like himself. The scene appears, in some manner, like enchanted Ground, owing to the association of the Idea of the Great Washington with every thing you behold. His vault, containing his remains, made a great impression on my mind. His widow is an affecting personage—dignified and polite, inspiring the greatest respect and veneration. She remembered and professed to be very glad to see me, which I doubt not, recollecting the great attachment which she knew most of the Army had for her husband.

After dinner I took my leave & received a kind

* Ogden was then a U. S. Senator.

(172)

invitation to pay her another visit, when it might be in my power. I promised to do so next winter.

My love to all to whom I bear it, & believe me to be continually yours.

AARON OGDEN.

Mrs. Aaron Ogden,
       Elizabeth Town,
                New Jersey.

SARAH ROBINSON.

NEW YORK,
30th of the Fourth Month,
1789.

I feel exceedingly mortified and hurt, my dear cousin, that so many of my letters to thee have been miscarried. I have certainly written as many as half a dozen since thee left New York, although thou acknowledgest the receipt of but one, which almost discourages me from making another attempt, so uncertain is it whether it will ever reach Brandywine, but I cannot entirely give it up, as I am sure they afford you some pleasure. I received thine of the 4th, and was pleased to hear you were well and that my dear uncle and aunt talked of making New York a visit. I shall wish for a wedding in the family often, if it will bring such good strangers; do, my dear, insist on it, and do not let

---

* Miss Sarah Robinson was the daughter of Rowland Robinson and Sarah Franklin. Kitty Franklin Wister, her cousin, to whom the letter is written, was the daughter of Casher Wister and Mary Franklin. Both Sarah Robinson and Mary Wister were sisters of Walter Franklin (the "Uncle Walter" referred to in this letter), one of whose daughters married De Witt Clinton, the other George Clinton.

them disappoint us; we promise ourselves a great enjoyment in their company. Uncle John's affair goes on rapidly and will soon come to a crisis, and he is as attentive a swain as thou wouldst wish to see, and as much delighted at the approaching event. Betsy and Polly are expected to-day. I hope they will be prudent, but no doubt it will be a great trial; they are all extremely averse to the match, and uncle has his hands full with them, thou may suppose. If I could but sit an hour with thee, my dear, how much I should have to tell thee, but it will not do to put all on paper; but so far I will say that the Widow would have nothing to say to Uncle John, until he would be reconciled to Cousin Tommy, in consequence of which he visits there and takes a great deal of notice of his three little granddaughters, a very pleasing event to all of us, and does great honour to our aunt, and endears her very much to me; she is, I think, every way suitable to our Uncle, and I have no doubt will make him an excellent wife. Billy is now out on his journey to Vermont; he has been gone eight weeks. I have frequently heard from him during his absence, but do not know when to expect him. Our dear little Eliza is now in the small-pox, and like to have it very favourably, a favour which demands our gratitude; the rest of the little tribe are well. My little neice Esther grows finely and her mother is as well as can be expected.

Great rejoicing in New York on the arrival of General Washington, an elegant barge decorated with an awning of satin, 12 oarsmen dressed in white frocks and blue ribbons, went down to E. Town last fourth day to bring him up. A stage was erected at the coffee house wharf, covered with a carpet for him to step on, where a company of light-horse, one of artillery, and most of the inhabitants were waiting to receive him. They paraded through Queen st. in great form, while the music of the drums and the ringing of the bells were enough to stun one with the noise. Previous to his coming Uncle Walter's* house on Cherry St. was taken for him, and every room furnished in the most elegant manner. Aunt Osgood and Lady Kitty Duer† had the whole management of it. I went the morning before the General's arrival to take a look at it, the best of furniture in every room and the greatest quantity of plate and china I ever saw, the whole of the first and second story is papered and the floors covered with the richest kind of Turkey and Wilton carpets. The house did honour to my Aunts and Lady Kitty; they spared no pains nor expense on it. Thou must

---

* Walter Franklin.

† William Alexander, Earl of Stirling, Major-General in the Continental Army, had two daughters, the second of whom, Catharine, married Col. William Duer, and was known as Lady Kitty Duer. (Duer's "*Life of Lord Stirling.*")

know that Uncle Osgood and Duer were appointed to procure a house and furnish it, accordingly they pitched on their wives as being likely to do it better. I have not yet done, yet my dear is thee not almost tired? The evening after his excellency's arrival, there was a general illumination took place, except among my friends (quakers), and those styled Anti-Federalists. The latter's windows suffered some, thou may imagine. As soon as the General has sworn in, a grand exhibition of fireworks is to be displayed, which it is expected is to be to-morrow. There is scarcely anything talked about now but General Washington and the palace, and of little else have I told thee yet, tho' I have spun my miserable scrawl already to a great length; but thou requested to know all that was going forward. I have just heard that William Titus of Woodbury is going to be married to a sister of Uncle Browne, mother to Thomas Browne, who I believe thee knows. Eliza Titus, her husband, and Father and Mother, spent the evening with me last sixth day. Eliza is much altered since I saw her, she is much thinner and plainer. Marie de Courcy, too, has been in town a fortnight; she made her home at Uncle Osgood's, but was a great deal among us all She is about making a little tour into Connecticut on a visit to a friend, Lucy Bull, with Joseph Bull, who is now in town. Our families are all well. Hettie is still with us. Rowland and the girls' love to you. Accept mine, my dear cousin, and write soon to thy affectionate cousin.

SARAH ROBINSON.

Kitty F. Wister.

BENJAMIN FRANKLIN BACHE.*

BENJAMIN FRANKLIN BACHE TO HIS FATHER, RICHARD BACHE.

[1775.]

My dear Papa, you'd give a guinea
Just now to see my nurse, Mo'minny,
With such a fretful busy face,
Pursuing me from place to place.
She scolds and coaxes, frowns and flatters,
And now she's dumb, and then she chatters,
And all, forsooth, to get me out,
With her to flirt and gad about!

---

* Sarah Franklin, the only daughter of Benjamin Franklin, married Richard Bache, a merchant of Philadelphia, on the 29th October, 1767, when her father was in England, fighting the reimposition of the Stamp Act upon the Colonies. The first child of this union was Benjamin Franklin Bache, born August 12, 1769. His grandfather's son, Governor William Franklin, stood one godfather at his christening, and a Mr. Brayton was proxy for Dr. Franklin, who was the other. In May, 1775, when Franklin returned from Europe, he found his godson a bright little boy of six years, the pet and pride of his mother and grandmother. The following year, when Franklin went to Paris as the envoy of the United States, he carried the boy with him, and had him educated in Paris and Geneva. Bache did not return to America until 1785, and in 1790 entered upon his brilliant and tempestuous career as editor of the Philadelphia *General Advertiser*, afterwards known as the *Aurora*. In this capacity he was the champion of Jefferson and his school, and, as much as any writer of his time, may be said to have shared

(179)

Now spare your labor, Goody Nurse;
For, look, says I, with all your fuss,
I won't be *coax'd* abroad, nor *carried*;
Go—coax your Sweetheart, and get married;
Then, please the pigs, I hope to see
Your Husband plague'd instead of me!
She persevered and I persisted;
The more I turn'd the more she twisted;
And truly I'm ashamed to say
What gave occasion for the fray:
In short, she made this mighty pother,
Lest I should interrupt my Mother,
While she was writing, Sir, to you!
No, no, let Benny scribble too;

---

in the formation of the Democratic party. He died suddenly during a yellow fever epidemic in Philadelphia, at the age of twenty-eight years.

It was the custom of his mother, when he was a child, to take refuge from the commotions which then beset Philadelphia in Burlington, a quiet retreat in New Jersey, where William Franklin had a residence, and it was from some place near there, and evidently just before Benjamin Franklin's return to America in 1775, that the poem was written. It has descended in a regular line in the Bache family, and its authenticity and antiquity are beyond question, but the penmanship is not that of a child of six, nor can its composition be reasonably attributed to so young a mind, however precocious it might be. In the published letters of Franklin and his family, there are many allusions to the brightness of "little Benny," but there is nothing to indicate such startling precociousness as this poem would indicate. The metre, it is true, is the easiest, and the thoughts are simple and child-like, but the whole betokens rather the combined effort of the witty and clever Sarah Bache and her clever little son, than the individual production of the latter.

Mamma, let Benny write.   She smiled,
And said I was a Charming Child;
And—here, says she, my lovely Ben,
My Franklin, take your Mother's pen,
And scribble what you will, my Boy,
I'm sure 'twill give your Father joy.
So Mollie was obliged to yield,
And like a Man, I kept the Field.

We've been to Burlington, and there
We made a progress through the Fair.
The Street was crouded full enough
With idle Folks and paltry stuff;
The Country People, far and near,
Flock here to market twice a year.
They think that something new and rare
Is to be seen at every Fair,
Some Curiosity;—but no,
'Tis they themselves that are the show.
But, had you seen us press along,
From Stall to Stall, through such a throng,
I think it would have made you proud
To see my courage in the Croud;
Take care, says I, make room for Benny,
Among the rest to spend his penny;
So, one I pull'd and push'd another,
And made a Passage for my Mother!
Among the trinkets to be bought
For eighteen pence—not worth a Groat—
I *must* upon a Fairing fix,
And so I chose a Coach and six.

At Burlington we stay'd some weeks,
And every day I stuffed my Cheeks
With Creams and dainties from the Dairy,
Besides the victuals dress'd by Mary.

We had the pleasure still to find
Our worthy Friends so very kind,
And every thing so good and clever,
I cou'd have wish'd to stay forever ;
But that, you know, wou'd never do
Without my Grandmamma and you.
And oh, Papa, why don't you come,
And spend your Christmas here at home ?
Had I but wings ! Oh, how romantic !
I'd soon fly over the Atlantic,
Salute my Grand Papa, and make
His Cheeks and sides with laughing ake,
And in my English Danma's breast,
Make for a while the Kingbird's nest,
And then return with you, Papa,
Again to bless my own Mamma.

But now, I've writ so long a letter,
I only wish it were a better!
I hope in time I shall improve
And more and more deserve your love.
Mamma takes all the pains she can
To make me good and be a man ;
'Tis her delight, she says, to teach
Your ever dutiful

BEN FRANKLIN BACHE.

GOVERNOR JOHN PAGE.

N. Y<u>k</u> MARCH 12<u>th</u> 1790.

My dear Mann :

Last night I received yours of 21<u>st</u> inst. from York, & was happy to find that you & the rest of my dear Family were well; but was sorry that the whooping cough had surrounded the dear little ones; that Disorder is more to be dreaded on their Acc<u>t</u> than the measles—but I hope in God neither will hurt them—I have sent on in different letters a pretty good collection of Garden seed, & will send any other you may want. For clover seed I find no conveyance. I would wish to get many things here & send to you if I had the money, but the Expensiveness of living & Lillys *take in* keep me poor indeed. I will send you the Books if to be had—I suppose your sisters have told you that I am

---

*John Page, of Rosewell, Gloucester Co., Va., was a member of the Committee of Safety and Lieutenant Governor of Virginia during the Revolution, beside which he raised a regiment of militia in his county. He was elected to Congress as soon as the Constitution was adopted, and served till 1797. In December, 1802, he was made Governor of Virginia. Appleton's *Cyclopædia of American Biography*. The above letter was written from Congress to his kinsman.

about to be married to Miss Lowther, I must refer you to them for my Description of that Lady, & of my Prospect of happiness. As I shall now keep Rosewell & consult my own Ease & Happiness rather than the Gratification of unreasonable impatient creditors & mean if possible at the Death of my Wife to give it to you, I wish you to have every thing done which can preserve the Buildings &c upon cheap terms & let me know what may be wanted for that purpose, possibly workmen may be hired here by the year—from Miss Lowther's Disposition toward me & my Family & her happy Temper I conceive it will be unnecessary for you & your family to be at any Expense or Inconvenience on Account of our Marriage, at any Rate as long as I shall be in Congress—Should I live to return & settle at Rosewell I will assist you to the utmost of my Power, & fix you in W^{ms}burg, Richmond, York or Gloucester, as you may think will best suit your Views—enclosed are some grains of the corn which Mr Willis desired me to get him an early sort—I have sent him the like Number & shall continue to send you both till I have sent the *Quart* which I have.

Give my Love to Betsey your Brothers & Sisters & all my Family & Friends; being called off I can only say that I am affec^{ty} yrs.

J. PAGE.

PETER MINOR.

PETER MINOR TO JOHN MINOR, JR.*

PETERSBURG, 25th Sept. 1783.

Dear Jack:

I now sit down to apologize for not answering your former Favours. In the 1st place I've been so very unwell For about Two months that I was Incapable of attending to Business. In the next, as soon as I was able to attend to my most principle Concerns I found affairs so behind hand that I could attend to nothing else But that, till I got them in tolerable way again, By which means I have neglected to answer my Friends Letters. It was not Inatention or forgetfulness, But the Situation I found my affairs in, so that I hope this will convince you it was not the want of Friendship, But nothing more than wishing to have matters in a good way.

You ought to know my dear Jack that when a man undertakes a piece of Business or Studies a profession, he ought to apply his whole time to it, or he may not be master of it till old age creeps

---

* He was in the Revolutionary Army and was afterwards a member of the Virginia Assembly.

on too far for him too do anything [MS torn] he cannot Injoy it with that Satisfaction had he [MS torn].

I mean my own Situation had it been agreed by my Friends to have allow'd me to chose what I now profess It would have been greatly to my Interest and (make no doubt to their) satisfaction. But our parents and Friends very seldom consult our inclinations tho perhaps it may be for our advantage.

I will inform you in my next what I have been doing here & what Intend to do in future, and at the same Time my dear Jack you'l Remember to inform me what you are doing &c. &c. and how you come on in your wise assembly. Your Bills pass'd & thrown out, motion made &c. &c. mind this Jack you must write me Two or three Letters to my one. That is allowing for my being absent or Business Interests. But this be assured of I will answer every Letter you write without some Accident; which I know you will Excuse.

As the old Gentleman may not allow you, or an opportunity may not offer for him to send you pocket cash Let me know and I will send you a few Guineas. But not to sport with Jack, mind that, a Gamster In my Idea is the most Despisable being that exists, at the same time I think a young Fellow ought not to be stinted in any Rasional pleasures.

As to you first Bill for the Emancipating Slaves I think it met with a very good fate for we might as well let Loose a parcel of Indians or Lions as to Let our Slaves free without they could be sent from the Continent.*

Your Second Bill I so far agree, that Emigration should be encouraged by every good member of Society as our Country is young & very extensive, And the greater number of Souls we have, the Richer we shall be—as to Exempting them from Taxes for three four or Five years, I think would be of no disadvantage to us, But rather an advantage, as it would Encourage Emigration. But as to admitting Foreigners to the Highest offices or to any office whatever, I think is very unpolitick and the Highest absurdity. You must see Instances every day of Scotchmen getting into offices who have Acted in a Lukewarm manner ever Since the war began, nay have Tried to Alienate the minds of the Ignorant part of mankind from what we have been so long Contending for. They

---

* "The disposition to emancipate them [the slaves] is strongest in Virginia. Those who desire it form, as yet, the minority of the whole State, but it bears a respectable proportion to the whole in numbers and weight of character, and it is continually recruiting by the addition of nearly the whole of the young men as fast as they come into public life. I flatter myself that it will take place there at some period of time not very distant." Thomas Jefferson, *Works*, Vol. IX., p. 290. The editor is unable to find any record of the bill referred to in this letter.

hang together, they are an artfull, Designing sett
of men, and were we once to admit them on the
same footing of our good Citizens who has fought
& Bled for their Country It would be unpolitick
and Reflecting on our Country that we were obliged
to be beholden to those very men (that would have
Cut our throats) to represent us. For God sake
never let it be said, that we were obliged to import
Scoundrels that has been fighting us and then to
come here and be admitted into offices. It would
be acknowledging that we had not Citizens capable
of that Trust. It will not bare reflection. For my
part I should be clear for excluding the first Gen-
eration from any publick service whatever and
none But Natives should Represent us [MS.
torn.]*

I have wrote you a long Scribble. I do not
know wheather you can make it out or not. I was
obliged to write in a hurry as Mr. Call is waiting.
I forgot you are a Lawyer, therefore you can Inter-
pret for the Best.

I an Dr Jack yr aff uncle

PETER MINOR.

* These criticisms may refer to the " Citizen bill." See *Letters of Joseph Jones, 110.*